"With a generous heart and stunning eye for detail, Travis has written an impeccably researched book that's indispensable for the beer lover."

—J. Ryan Stradal, *New York Times* bestselling author of *The Lager Queen of Minnesota* and *Kitchens of the Great Midwest*

"Encouraging wanderlust and wonderment, Michael Travis has written a travelogue here that will surely entice readers to hit the road and veer towards the nearest (and farthest) reaches of the state for a pint of great Kansas beer!"

—Geoff Deman, Head Brewer, Free State Brewing Company, Lawrence, Kansas

"To me, this book is about more than microbreweries. It's about the story of people and meshing their passion of making beer with giving their community a place for people to connect."

—Marci Penner, Co-Founder and Executive Director, Kansas Sampler Foundation, Inman, Kansas

"It is a book about the towns and cities of Kansas, and about Kansans who are passionate about their brews, written with enthusiasm and love for these subjects. This book is a fun resource for planning your road trip around the great state of Kansas."

—Jennifer M. Kassebaum, Owner, Flint Hills Books, Council Grove, Kansas

CELEBRATING
KANSAS
BREWERIES

People, Places & Stories

MICHAEL J. TRAVIS

AMERICAN PALATE

Published by American Palate
A Division of The History Press
Charleston, SC
www.historypress.com

First published 2022

Manufactured in the United States

ISBN 9781467151924

Library of Congress Control Number: 2022936626

The people can be depended upon to meet any national crisis.
The great point is to bring them the real facts, and beer.

—Abraham Lincoln

To Ivy, the love of my life, who embodies all the good things in this world. You are my everything—yesterday, today and for all tomorrows.

CONTENTS

ACKNOWLEDGEMENTS

I had no idea how many people would become part of my book community when I started the brewery road trip in June 2021. As I traveled state highways throughout Kansas, the prairie sun overhead in all its glory, I had to contend with the cloud cover of the pandemic. I am speechless when I realize that I met more people and made more friends in 2021 than I have in my entire life, despite the raging pandemic and its pitfalls.

I am so thankful that I have the wonderful family I do. Everything starts with my wife, Ivy, who has been next to me since I talked aloud about this dream. Ivy is my rock, my selfless angel who has carried such a heavy weight for us as a couple for years. I must confess that my life journey has been littered with broken dreams that were short-lived, resulting from my inability to fully commit and cross the finish line. Despite the disappointments Ivy and my family have witnessed, the love and support that has come my way have made me a rich man.

As I planned my approach to the visits, the travel and the timeline to complete the project, I reached out to family and friends, looking for volunteers to join me for brewery visits. I look back at the memories of my wife and girls accompanying me on separate occasions and have heart smiles. I laugh aloud about Ivy taking a siesta on the patio of Manhattan Brewing Company after endorsing all its high-ABV styles! I cherish the life moments I had with my youngest daughter, Meaghan, who is as intense a craft beer fan as I am. Together, with my granddaughter Luna Grace joining us, we sat on patios, enjoying flights and celebrating family. I chuckle and wrap my eldest daughter, Katie, in my arms as I reminisce about our time together in Sterling, Hutch and Wichita. Close encounters with ostriches were followed by falling for Third Place Brewery and Tom Kryzer, who hosted us as the publican of the place.

I must thank the ten-point buck that surprised me, as I did him, one night at dusk for his skill at keeping his speed up and glancing off my right fender, moving safely off the road as I stayed on the road.

I traveled innumerable miles with a good friend who visited more breweries with me than anyone else. Kevin Lorenz, my in-law, loves a road trip as much as I do. I cannot thank him enough for his driving, his humor, his heart and our growing friendship that became more meaningful as the conversations and tasters accumulated.

I save this space to salute a friend, a classmate, who flew from New Hampshire to Kansas City, intent on reconnecting with me after four decades. I am humbled by Brad Stevens and his longstanding effort to keep us connected. The weekend we had together was full of flights, pints and his first visit to the K. Of course, the weekend was planned around a Royals home series against his beloved Red Sox. Brad, I look forward to taking a ride in your 1930 Model A to 603 Brewery in Londonderry, New Hampshire, next time I visit my childhood home.

The brewing community across the Sunflower State has been so welcoming to this aspiring writer and his passion project. I have spent close to one hundred hours immersed in relaxed, inspiring and happy conversations with the owners and brewers (often the same person) along the way. The energy I have brought to the table each visit has been overwhelmed by the passion, commitment and dedication these people have about their dream, their craft beer and serving and supporting their communities.

I deeply appreciate Phil Kasper, program director at KCLY/KFRM in Clay Center, for being the first to call me an author while on his radio show, *On the Front Porch*. Not only did Phil give me the opportunity to establish my voice, but he also gave me confidence in myself soon after the outset of my book journey.

I want to make special mention of a *New York Times* bestselling author in the writing community, J. Ryan Stradal, who wrote *The Lager Queen of Minnesota*.[1] He graciously has given me counsel, tips and feedback along the way.

I benefited from the wisdom that my older brother, Mark, provided. He shared book contracts he had for books such as *My Brave Boys*, providing me the opportunity to understand and appreciate the importance of landing with the right editor and publisher for my book. Mark has always been there for me. His brotherly love and cheerleading from Canterbury, New Hampshire, will be cherished.

Every moment that I spend at my writing desk, a framed e-mail from Chad Rhoad, of Arcadia Publishing and The History Press, looks down at me. Chad took an interest in my project through the publisher's internal review and shared the great news that my book was approved for publication on an early November morning. Chad, you do not know the impact you have had on me and my dream of becoming a writer. You gave me the courage to believe in myself.

It is time to thank two people, one a partner and the other my son-in-law, for their tireless dedication and efforts to support my writing. Christy Schneider, owner of Inkello Letterpress and Yellow Pencil Studio in East Lawrence, is a partner who I hope becomes a lifelong friend. Her creative talents, ability to understand my thoughts, translating them through her design lens and offering incredible counsel as a children's author and illustrator have had such an influence on my work. Christy, thank you for your gentle challenges, belief in my project and support along the way.

Chris Orlando, my son-in-law, has been knee-deep in my writing since day one. Chris, who has a doctorate in education, blesses Southwest Middle School eighth graders in Lawrence through his passion to help young people learn and grow, while also serving as my editor. I will forever remember the excitement as a writer when I would see a piece come back from him with the comment, "This is a good story. Here you go! Not many edits on this one." I felt like I was punched in the nose often, initially buoyant that I had made muster, followed by the sudden loss of air in my lungs, as I counted the number of callouts I needed to ponder. Chris, your diplomacy, challenges and courage to beat up your father-in-law daily for the last six months is to be admired.

I have been deeply vested in the people, as well as their stories I have listened to along the way. Talented people are doing incredible things in our state. The risk-taking, tireless commitment and belief that their dreams could come true have made me pause frequently. These people have built vibrant communities that will have a lasting impact on their towns and our state. The magic that I have tried my best to capture in this book comes alive through the following Irish toast, which illustrates how a brewery and its community can feel like family, waiting to listen, support and celebrate life together. I raise my glass and express my gratitude to all who I have mentioned, and those who I have not, who played a part in making my dream come true.

For every wound, a balm.
For every sorrow, cheer.
For every storm, a calm.
For every thirst, a beer.[2]

Cascade hops maturing on bine prior to Kansas Hop Company harvest. I toured the three-acre hopyard with co-owner Ryan Triggs. *Author's collection.*

INTRODUCTION

I wrote my first book when I was nine years old. I captured the experiences that I shared with my two brothers, sister and parents as we drove to the West Coast and back in our blue VW bus during the summer of '72. If you were to turn the pages in my spiral-bound school notebook, you would see how I captured each day's adventure through taping a collage of postcards, gift bags and brochures on a page, leaving room for my thoughts. I printed passages with my trusty pencil highlighting the best hotel, the eighty-five-cent Howard Johnson's parfait, the Pikes Peak chipmunks and the famous Utah bumbleberry pie. I love my mom for opening my eyes to the joy of writing about things I love. The summer of '72 journal experience inspired me to write about a new journey someday in the future.

Jumping ahead fifty years, I am celebrating the publication of my first book! My hope is that you will feel like you have taken the journey with me across our wonderful state, stopping in thirty-seven towns blessed to have breweries in their communities. I have fallen in love with every corner of our Sunflower State while traveling twenty-eight consecutive weeks. I have visited fifty-nine breweries,[1] some multiple times, witnessing eleven that are in different phases of opening.

I thought that the book would be all about beer. Breweries offer us the chance to create an experience, see old friends and make new acquaintances. My focus shifted as I worked to capture the heartbeat of each brewery and its community. As the owners and brewers told their

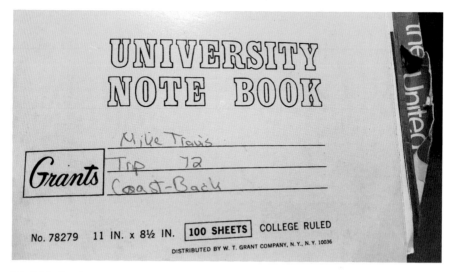

My "Trip '72 Coast—Back" journal, updated daily with comments regarding the miles we drove, the cities we saw and the memories. *Author's collection.*

stories, the communities created and the incredible people encountered migrated to the forefront of the story.

I hope that this book will serve as a motivation to go on brewery trips, whether afternoon or weekend escapes. Use each trip section to assist mapping out which breweries to see. Think about writing down dates for new beer releases or festivals that you cannot miss. Hopefully, you will continue to explore the state and the hidden gems within it, knowing that you are supporting innovative breweries working hard to establish themselves as a vibrant part of communities from Dodge City to Washington.

#CelebratingCommunityPeopleBeer

Enjoy the human-interest stories celebrating our brewery community that open each chapter. I valued writing the first feature, which focuses on a brewer's pursuit of a 2,500-year-old Egyptian recipe. The story, called "Brew Like an Egyptian," follows. It is an impressive example of a brewer challenging his artistry, motivated to give you something new to try.

The last feature story, "It's a Small Town Sticking Around," is the most important story that I wrote. The trend emerging in our state, led by young entrepreneurs going home to rural Kansas communities to open breweries, is both heartwarming and critical to the health and vibrancy of not only those rural towns but also our state.

I cannot wait to meet you at a Kansas brewery in the fall of 2022 as we celebrate the great people and the spirited communities that inspired this journey. Look for me at a nearby brewery, sharing stories with the owner or brewer, laughing and waiting to enjoy a pint with you, your friends and the brewery family. Cheers!

Adam Rosdahl, co-owner and head brewer at Norsemen Brewing Company in Topeka, Kansas. We enjoyed a pint while learning about Adam's pursuit of Egyptian beer. *Author's collection.*

Chapter 1

BREW LIKE AN EGYPTIAN

A terrible fire raged in the harbor of Alexandria, Egypt, close to 2,100 years ago. Set by order of Julius Caesar, as he and his forces laid siege, the blaze spread into the city. The Library of Alexandria[1] held an unprecedented number of scrolls and attracted the most brilliant thinkers of the time. The library was the glory of the ancient world, devastated by flames that destroyed priceless works, including the last twenty-six pages of the Hymn of Demeter.

"People like stories," Adam Rosdahl,[2] co-owner and head brewer at Norsemen Brewing Company, said to me as he talked about the elusive search for the missing ingredients, which were included in the twenty-six pages of the Hymn of Demeter. For Adam, it started as he began to read *The Immortality Key*, by Brian C. Muraresku.[3] As Adam progressed through the book, he found himself digging into Greek mythology. He was intrigued by the historical gathering of village leaders each September, in a town called Lucis, where they would embark on a spiritual journey. The participants celebrated the end of their fast, sleep-deprived and thirsty, by drinking an ancient beer called *kykeon* to bring the journey to a close. It is widely believed that *kykeon* was a psychoactive compounded brew. Participants, including Homer, experienced altered states of mind. At this point in our conversation, Adam paused, saying, "This recipe can be brewed without the bad stuff!"[4]

How can a brewer like Adam unearth the ingredients used more than two thousand years ago by Egyptian and Greek brewers? The improvements made in the science of archaeology allow researchers the ability to analyze organic residue evident in the fermented beverage vessels, whether intact or in shards. Adam found himself at a crossroads, with one path providing the first three ingredients that were used in *kykeon* through reading the pages still in existence of the Hymn of Demeter. The amazing strides made in the ability to analyze remnants of fermenting vessels from this time have offered a confusing array of spectrometer readings. Adam found himself looking at the second path, which was littered with possible ingredients including okra, sage, peas, compressed fruit, wine and even unwashed wool!

Adam is positioned to make the best decisions when honoring the ancient brewing history, with his own contemporary brewing processes and forward-looking artistry. It was clear to Adam that he knew what the fourth ingredient was. "It makes complete sense that they would have used honey. They would have added the mint and honey to make the beverage palatable." Adam went on to say, with horror, that simply soaking ground barley in hot water "will not taste good!"[5]

We all know that beer would be nowhere without key ingredients such as barley and water. To stay true to the ancient brewing process, Adam had to attempt to re-create Egyptian water. Securing ingredients that were authentic to this period took him to Massachusetts, where he found a group of guys who had harvested a strain of Egyptian barley that they were in the process of malting. He was hopeful that he could secure a bag of this unique barley, while reaching out to breweries such as Central Standard Brewing in Wichita, to obtain the right strain of wild fermentation ale yeast to use in the brewing of his version of *kykeon*.

One of the hurdles brewers must clear when pursuing these ancient recipes is to gain clearance from the FDA to use a new ingredient. Thanks to the efforts of Sam Calagione at Dogfish Head Brewery, most obscure ingredients from ancient recipes have been presented and approved. Debates continue to unfold over the use of mind-altering ingredients in this process, including ergot, which is a fungus that could have been on the grain, in this case barley. If this was what influenced the spiritual journey many experienced over several thousand years, the fact that ergot contains an acid that is known to be a precursor for the synthesis of LSD is alarming. At this point in our conversation, Adam shifted from the nonstarter of ergot as an ingredient and went on to share, "Some kinds of mint get you going like caffeine. There is a hypothesis that those drinking *kykeon*, while incredibly sleep- and food-deprived, could have gone cuckoo from an overload of alcohol coupled with a caffeine high."[6]

By the time you read this story, this beer might have moved through one of his seven-barrel vessels. When it hits the taps at Norsemen Brewing in Topeka, Adam will be creative with his messaging for this unique style. He knows that he cannot sit with every customer who walks through the doors to tell them about the style, the history and the expectations one should have as they take a first sip. "The trick is to get a year's worth of research into the attention span of someone who wants to drink a beer!"[7]

His passion and commitment to brew great beer is intrinsic to the approach the thirteen brewers in the "Wichita Way" chapter honor. This is a great area to go brewery hopping, with thirteen within 115 miles of one another, the bull's-eye of Wichita complemented by Hutch and five other towns. In the brewery chapter, you will have the opportunity to read about these brewers sharing their passion for the art and the joy they receive when serving their communities. Adam looks for any opportunity to talk shop, share best practices and enjoy a pint with brewers such as Torrey Lattin at Hopping Gnome Brewing Company, Ian Crane at Central Standard Brewing and Dan Norton of Norton's Brewing Company. Get out, have a pint and celebrate what they do.

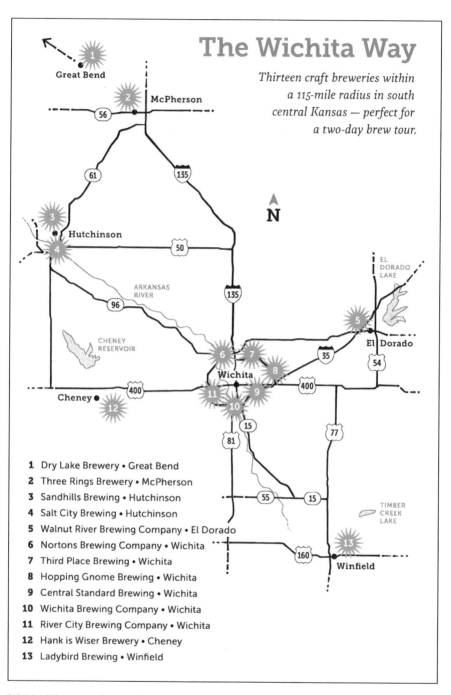

The Wichita Way

Thirteen craft breweries within a 115-mile radius in south central Kansas — perfect for a two-day brew tour.

N

1 Dry Lake Brewery • Great Bend
2 Three Rings Brewery • McPherson
3 Sandhills Brewing • Hutchinson
4 Salt City Brewing • Hutchinson
5 Walnut River Brewing Company • El Dorado
6 Nortons Brewing Company • Wichita
7 Third Place Brewing • Wichita
8 Hopping Gnome Brewing • Wichita
9 Central Standard Brewing • Wichita
10 Wichita Brewing Company • Wichita
11 River City Brewing Company • Wichita
12 Hank is Wiser Brewery • Cheney
13 Ladybird Brewing • Winfield

Wichita Way map. *Courtesy of Christy Schneider, Inkello Design & Letterpress, East Lawrence, Kansas.*

Chapter 2

THE WICHITA WAY

1. DRY LAKE BREWING

1305 Main * Great Bend, Kansas 67530
620-793-0400
www.drylakebeer.com/home
www.facebook.com/DryLakeBeer
Brewing System: 5BBL

Ryan and Kevin are a perfect match for Dry Lake Brewing. Ryan Fairchild is the dreamer, who is all in when committed to a new passion project and does not respond well to being told that something cannot be done. Kevin Buckley is the conservative partner, an eternal pessimist who typically does not jump into ventures with reckless abandon. Ryan has taken on huge projects like the first year of BikeBrewQ[1] (a bicycling, brew fest and barbecue event supporting the Cystic Fibrosis Foundation) with just thirty days to pull it all together. Ryan delivered the first year and celebrated the sixth annual event in 2021. Ryan took homebrewing to a new level by growing hops in his backyard. As the years passed, the three hop varieties were threatening to take over the entire yard. Kevin is the guy who was homebrewing in his driveway years ago when a police officer pulled up in front of his house because a neighbor called, concerned that he was running a meth lab.

Dry Lake Brewing tap menu in Ryan Fairchild and Kevin Buckley's Great Bend, Kansas brewery. *Author's collection.*

Their balancing act was critical in the initial stages of the brewery journey. A local business couple considering retirement approached, asking them, "If you take the finances out of the picture, why aren't you opening a brewery?" A mutual friend facilitated a meeting Ryan and Kevin had with this potential investor. "Okay, we are opening a brewery,"[2] Ryan said when they walked out of that initial meeting.

Within a week, the team had bought a building on Main Street that had just been vacated by Brown Shoe Fit. Ryan quipped that "we owned seven thousand square feet of maroon" as they came to an agreement on an offer for the building. The two forged a unique path, considering they bought a building before writing a business plan or bringing investors on board. As with many of the brewery stories in the state, Kevin and Ryan started putting their sweat equity into the space while holding full-time jobs. Eventually, Kevin was able to go full-time at the brewery to make it happen; Ryan has continued to hold his other position while staying involved in local economic development, Cystic Fibrosis Foundation fundraising event management and being the facilities and grain operator at his brewery.

Their dream became reality in late spring 2021 when Dry Lake Brewing opened its doors. Ryan and Kevin reminisced about growing up in the Great Bend area, thinking back to the days when someone "was in" if they were members out at Barton Lake. The lake dried up when the dam was removed years ago. As they brainstormed about the naming of the brewery, they realized that Dry Lake was perfect because it gave a nod to that area in Barton County while also underscoring their goal of becoming the place to hang out in Great Bend.

Kevin oversees everything from brewing to managing the books to daily duties such as cleaning the lines. The space they designed is planned and positioned for growth when that day comes. They built the brewhouse in the middle with the fermenters in a circle to increase efficiencies. Kevin has built the style offering at Dry Lake starting with the 5-0 Wheat, named after the day the police officer pulled up to witness those origins of the flagship beer brewing in the driveway. Kevin mentioned that he was fortunate to learn from others in the early days, such as Larry Cook, owner and master brewer at Dodge City Brewing. He spent a day in Dodge, brewing, cleaning tanks and gaining an appreciation for the importance of the daily nurturing of the beer as it fermented.

When you look at the sky, the spark you might see just above the horizon is the "spark that lights downtown up" in Great Bend. Make a point of stopping in at Dry Lake, meeting Ryan and Kevin and hanging out with friends while enjoying a pint. The sign painted on the wall leading into the brewery, "BEER," is simply said and so true. Trust me, follow the arrow.

2. THREE RINGS BREWERY & TAPROOM

536 Old U.S. 81 * McPherson, Kansas 67460
620-504-5022
www.threeringsbrewery.com
www.facebook.com/threeringsbrewery
Brewing System: 7BBL

Three Rings Brewery, McPherson, Kansas. *Courtesy of Three Rings Brewery.*

Three Rings Brewery & Taproom, co-owned by a father-and-son team, has brewing lineage that stretches back twelve generations to Einbeck, Germany. Berend Brauer, Brian Smith's (co-owner) twelfth-great-grandfather, was the brewmaster of Einbeck in the early 1500s.[3] Berend the brewmaster had a fan, Martin Luther,[4] who later in life was a priest, theologian, author and composer.

Luther, at the age of seventeen, entered the University of Erfurt, 119 miles southeast of Einbeck. Martin described the university less than favorably early in his academic career, calling it a beerhouse and whorehouse. He graduated in 1505 with a fondness for beer, which led him to Einbeck and Berend Brauer. Twenty years after he graduated, Luther requested a cask of beer from Berend for his wedding celebration. Legend notes that Martin enjoyed the Brauer family beer from his three-ringed stein, which he used while visiting the brewery in Einbeck.

Brian and his son Ian decided to pay homage to the family's centuries-old brewing tradition by naming their brewery Three Rings. Today, the brewery is thriving, celebrating its fifth anniversary in June 2021. The day I visited, I noticed two medals framed and on display in the brewery. Ian proudly told me that they had won their first two national awards in the Can Can 2021 Festival, the only fest supporting canned beer breweries.

Ian's brewing journey was inspired by a tour he experienced at the Fort Collins Anheuser-Busch Biergarten and production facilities after making a college visit to Colorado State University. He surprised his dad, sharing his excitement not about becoming a Ram but instead telling his dad, "I want to make beer."[5]

He graduated from K-State, focused on learning as much as he could about fermenting as he worked toward his food science degree. Ian started hustling at that point, looking for the brewery door that he could wedge open for his first opportunity.

After learning that he did not get the Boulevard internship he had applied for, Ian called the brewmaster thirty minutes later to ask what he needed to do to reverse the rejections that were piling up. He earned his way into a half-internship as part of the quality-control team, having impressed brewmaster

Steve Pauwels with his determination. The Boulevard experience opened doors for him at Tallgrass Brewing in Manhattan, where he was head of its quality control over a four-year period.

During the beginning of Ian's brewing career, he and his dad started homebrewing. "Practice makes perfect,"[6] Ian said about their homebrewing days. Brian and Ian decided that it was time to open a taproom and share their beer with the community. The day I visited, Three Rings was busy with regulars coming in for growler refills, families spending time together while mom and dad could have a pint and folks ending a workday with a pint and bar seat. Ian has twelve beers on tap, brewing everything from an easy-drinking blonde ale to a whiskey barrel stout. He and his dad keep the taps fresh by introducing close to half a dozen seasonal brews per year to complement the four core beers, which include my favorite, the Wanderlust Scottish red.

The duo love going back in history, trying to brew what their ancestors did, experimenting, for example, with smoke beers. They are also supporting future farming ideas such as development of a perennial wheat grass, called kernza. This winter-hardy wheat, with a root system that reaches depths of ten feet, will have a positive impact on our earth, reducing erosion, nutrient runoff and providing a year-round cover. Three Rings was one of the first breweries in our state to experiment, brewing its first beer using kernza wheat.

Brian's great-grandfather carried the last name Brauer, meaning brewer in German. Berend no doubt is proud of what Brian and Ian are serving to their loyal customers and new adventurers at Three Rings Brewery. *Prost!*

3. SANDHILLS BREWING

111 West 2nd Avenue * Hutchinson, Kansas 67501
620-244-9782
sandhillsbrewing.com
www.facebook.com/sandhillsbrewinghutch
Brewing System: 3½BBL

This is a delightful story about twin brothers—as well as best friends—who grew up in the close-knit Williamson family amid the Sand Hills. Each child in the family was given a name linked to nature, with Pippin and Jonathan honoring varieties of apples. Their deep appreciation of the natural environment no doubt grew as they spent lazy summer afternoons exploring the dunes, trails and grassland prairie for which the Sand Hills are famous. That love is on exhibit today, shining through at their breweries. This visit for me was all about family as well, which was fitting considering what I was learning. My oldest daughter, Katie Grace, was making her first of two brewery visits on an overnight trek to Sterling, Hutchinson and Wichita.

Why are there two locations? It comes back to the love the two brothers have for each other and where they live. They have had symmetrical professional journeys, both owning and leading online gaming companies. They even opened the location in Mission one year later to the day than in Hutchinson. The brewery business has kept Pippin in Hutch and Jonathan in KC while minimizing the miles separating the two, as they are in constant daily contact while managing the business.

Two brothers, two locations and, in ways, two unique audiences. The Chickadee Berliner Weisse is the top beer in Hutch, while the Junco New England IPA is the pint of choice in the Mission location. Both styles celebrate different bird species, as do all core beers in the Sandhills lineup. Count on Sandhills to stretch your taste buds with an array of barrel-aged beers. Top of the list for the team today is a passion for oak-aged beer that they discovered as they watched brewers experiment with oak-aged pilsners. Rest assured that the brothers strive to have an option available for whatever your palate leans toward, including a barrel-aged style on any day you visit.

What I found striking about the approach Pippin and Jonathan share has been their purpose-driven focus on building a brewery business that will last for decades to come. Sandhills Brewing will age well because of the discipline they have brought over from their other businesses. Consistency for customers when any of the eight taps are pulled is essential. Pippin went on to share, "More than anything, if you want to be somewhere long-term, you have to start planning for that early on. It's the overall mindset, thinking long-term so you can make better, more thoughtful decisions that is important."[7]

When you visit Sandhills on a Friday or Saturday, ask the team if they have a test batch on tap. The brothers admired a model that the Side Projects Brewery[8] in Maplewood, Missouri, implemented that has helped shape the character and life of the Show-Me State brewery. There, customers can buy beer with the label "Shared Brew," which means staff brewed the beer on open equipment between their regular brewing. Pippin talked about the ability anyone on his staff has to make a beer with their five-gallon

My daughter Katie with a flight of Sandhills Brewing tasters. This was her first visit with her dad on the Hutchinson and Wichita trip. *Author's collection.*

homebrewing equipment. However, there's one rule in place: "a beer that sucks will go right down the drain."[9]

When the staff buys in to the culture created at Sandhills, it empowers and enables the team to be a more intrinsic part of the brewery. The energy created collectively will strengthen the efforts the twins are making to ensure that Sandhills is on the Kansas brewery landscape for a long time.

4. SALT CITY BREWING COMPANY

514 North Main * Hutchinson, Kansas 67501
620-888-5326
saltcitybrewing.com
www.facebook.com/saltcitybrewing
Brewing System: 10BBL

Shortly after I sat down to enjoy a pint and dinner at Salt City Brewing Company, located on North Main Street, Cole Petermann introduced himself. Cole, head brewer and son of Steven Petermann, who owns the brewery, exuded an amazing energy and assuredness. I connect the name Cole with the Wild West, picturing a sheriff walking slowly down Main Street, calming the nerves of those in town. Salt City has Cole at the helm of the brewhouse, pouring his heart into every brew he makes. Cole caught my attention when he said, "This is my village."[10]

Salt City Brewing draws in a community that loves the openness of the brewery. Friends and family can bask under the Kansas sunshine on a great patio, enjoying a pint, conversation and laughter. As the sun fell toward the horizon, the regulars took over the bar seats, checking in on one another and the latest happenings in Hutch. The tap offering is broad and balanced between core, small-batch and seasonal styles. Cole is focused on presenting beer styles that stay true to their lineage. If you want a classic style, Salt City Brewing is your destination. Steven and Cole think about the salt mines daily as they use filtration techniques to refine the water quality, which plays a huge part in delivering great beer.

Hutchinson, nicknamed "Salt City," is known for its historic operation of rock salt mining, which Hutchinson Salt Company established in 1923. The science behind building the mine, which is 650 feet below the surface and 980 acres in size, is immense. The underground salt museum, the "Strataca,"[11] required a shaft to be drilled through one of the largest aquifers in the world to create space for the site. The techniques used to protect the Ogallala Aquifer, which spreads through eight states, resulted in drilling progressing 15 feet at a time!

Next time you are in Hutchinson, I encourage you to check out the Strataca Museum. Amazingly, it's home to the original camera negatives from classic movies such as *Gone with the Wind* and *Ben-Hur*.

Salt City Brewing Company was the brainchild of Steven, who started his career in geology and Kansas oil and then discovered a passion for craft beer. His fascination for what elements were underground shifted with an obsession for craft beer and its four key ingredients, studying and homebrewing as he fine-tuned his craft.

The Petermanns have injected a vibe and energy on Main Street in Hutch that is growing. The day after I visited, they announced the purchase of another building adjacent to the brewery. The team is considering options for the space, which no doubt will benefit the brewhouse as well as provide opportunities for anything from more event space to a potential distillery.

Salt City was built to produce classic brews to quench the thirst of the after-work crowd. I encourage you to enjoy a great brew next time you are in the neighborhood.

5. WALNUT RIVER BREWING COMPANY

111 West Locust Avenue * El Dorado, Kansas 67042
316-351-8086
walnutriverbrewing.com
www.facebook.com/walnutriverbrewing
Brewing System: 30BBL

"Do what you love, because life is short," B.J. Hunt,[12] Walnut River's business operations leader and co-owner, said to me as we stood next to the brewery, watching a homebrew competition come alive. We were fortunate that the early December morning was comfortably crisp, under blue skies. I was enjoying the brewery's flagship beer, the Warbeard Irish red ale, as we settled in for a conversation, which spilled over to include the homebrewers participating in the event.

The camaraderie among the homebrewers was contagious. I made a point of checking in with each of the dozen or so homebrewers who had selected their go-to brew or had taken a leap of faith, excited to brew in uncharted territory, eventually handing over their beer to the Walnut River judges. They were competing to have the chance to have their recipe produced, packaged and sold by Walnut River Brewing Company. Hunt and Jay Sanderson, director of sales and marketing, told me that this was one of the two days that they were hosting homebrewers for the competition.

Walnut River Brewing Company taproom. *Courtesy of Walnut River Brewing Company, El Dorado.*

This community of homebrewers represents the essence of the birth of breweries in our state and across the country. Walnut River and the journey that Rick Goehring, co-owner and head brewer, embarked on epitomizes the path that homebrewers take to go professional, bringing craft beer in their new brewery to beer fans in a community such as El Dorado.

He worked in corporate IT for years, but the work left him restless and unfulfilled. Rick spent close to twenty years homebrewing, often on Saturdays, where his wife saw him at his happiest. Recognition came his way, as he won regional and national homebrew competitions. His story is like so many brewers across the state. With his wife's support, the two held hands and made the jump.

Rick slowly brought back to life a historic building that was in terrible condition. Its first brick had been laid in 1917. He built an apartment in the middle of the brewery for his family and lived amid controlled chaos as the team completed the taproom and small brewhouse. Rick was introduced to B.J., who also wanted to open a brewery. Once B.J. tasted his first beer brewed by Rick, Walnut River Brewing was destined to come alive. The ownership team also includes Travis Rohrberg, who in addition to his packaging and lab ownership at Walnut River has also been a supporter of the Ladybird Brewing team.

I was drawn to Thomas Derstein, one of the homebrewers, because rumor had it that he was brewing on Larry Cook's original equipment. Larry, owner and master brewer at Dodge City Brewing, took a journey similar to Rick's. I started a conversation with Thomas, wondering to myself if he would be the next homebrewer to take the leap, finding a home in the Sunflower State to fulfill his dream.

Thomas showed me Larry's original equipment as he brewed a Black IPA. He had homebrewed for two years, catching the bug, setting up his brewhouse in half of the garage. Derstein was smart, sharing with me that the first beer he brewed was a sour, knowing that his wife liked sours. With her support, he has been on the brewing journey, bottling new styles and heading to Dodge City Brewing to order a pizza and share his beer with Larry, who would take the time to give him feedback ranging from process tips to ingredients that he might want to consider. Thomas said, "Everyone here today seems to know Larry Cook, who always makes time for us."[13]

B.J. passionately shared the following life lesson, appreciating how it shaped his journey to Walnut River: "Every year that you work, you damn well better be doing what you want to do. You won't be taking any of it with you."[14] Could Thomas, winner of the inaugural Walnut River homebrew contest, become a professional brewer in the future? A giant step for him starts at Walnut River, where his Black IPA recipe was brewed in El Dorado and released for sale in April 2022.

6. NORTONS BREWING COMPANY

125 St. Francis * Wichita, Kansas 67202
316-425-9009
nortonsbrewing.com
www.facebook.com/nortonsbrewingcompany
Brewing System: 15BBL

"Everybody's singular goal is to grow Wichita breweries and have Wichita on people's minds when they think about a destination brewery city,"[15] Dan Norton, OG janitor at Nortons, told me. When I think of Wichita and the craft brewery community, I see the community coming first, the individual breweries second. The people of this brewing community in Wichita are always there for one another and are hopeful that there will be further brewery growth in the city. Dan is mentoring an assistant brewer, Aaron Hill, who has plans to open a taproom brewery by the end of 2022. "What I love to see now is all the younger generations getting into craft beer too,"[16] Dan said. He wants to see the growth in Wichita, stoked that the culture in the city will become richer.

Dan began his journey back in 2001 at River City Brewing Company and has made his mark in the Wichita craft beer industry. He transformed the brewery at River City, tripling the number of taps and eliminating guest taps such as Bud Light, now offering sixteen RCB styles. His journey to River City was a long one, as he tried to find the passion and profession that fit. At River City, "I finally found a subject I loved learning about."[17] Once he opened Nortons with his wife, Becky, he left traditional American styles in the rearview mirror, pushing his brewhouse team to have fun with brewing. Dan wanted weird styles, exploring and using different ingredients as he pushed the flavor envelope.

When you head to Nortons for a pint, you can pursue rich flavors and incredible combinations of ingredients across the majority of its twelve taps. If you lean traditional, know that Dan has come full circle, missing the old traditional styles that made him fall in love with craft beer. His

Taps at Nortons Brewing Company in Wichita, Kansas. *Author's collection.*

grandpa brewed and introduced Dan to the world of beer. He also learned to appreciate great beer while growing up in Coldwater, Michigan, with Bell's Brewery beer available in his hometown. He looked across the table at me and said, "There will forever be a place for those styles."[18] My first pint during our conversation was a classic West Coast IPA. Dan laughed as he said to me, "I figure you are old enough to remember those."[19]

The spirit and heartbeat at Nortons originate with Dan and Becky, who began dreaming of opening a brewery on evenings when they relaxed on their porch with a beer. Dan passionately believes in destiny and gets emotional when talking about how much fun he and Becky have working at their brewery. He shared that over the last three years, they have, in fact, grown closer in the process. Becky grew up with parents who were independent business owners. She caught the bug, as Dan did with brewing, and excelled in school at Friends University. Her business management and accounting backgrounds are essential to the success of their brewery.

"It's a goddamn miracle,"[20] Dan shared as he talked about his and Becky's dream taking shape after a long journey, celebrating their third anniversary in April 2021. Becky and Dan have a blast working together in a space that they and their team have poured their souls into. For the first time in our conversation, Dan's mood shifted as he choked up, reflecting about the people who work at Nortons and how hard they have worked to make it a success. What you experience at Nortons is a true reflection of who Dan and Becky are. "The main thing we set out to do is to show our kids what hard work and dedication can get you."[21] Dan knows from experience that finding what you love to do and figuring out how to make it a career is like getting a new lease on life.

7. THIRD PLACE BREWING

630 East Douglas Avenue * Wichita, Kansas 67202
316-833-2873
www.thirdplacebrew.com
www.facebook.com/ThirdPlaceBrewing
Brewing System: 1½BBL

> *publican (noun): the keeper of an inn or public house; one licensed to retail beer, spirits or wine.*
>
> *pub (noun): a place, especially in Great Britain or Ireland, where alcoholic drinks can be bought and drunk and where food is often available.*

Third Place Brewing is the closest thing to an English pub in Kansas. If you want to be in a true pub environment and have a lengthy conversation with a publican, this is your place. My oldest daughter, Katie, joined me for this memorable visit with Tom Kryzer, owner and brewer/recipe creator. I had a hunch that during our visit Third Place Brewing was going to offer more than just a pint of beer. The experience stayed true to a statement on its site: "In the beginning, there was beer. We liked beer. We began brewing beer. And in that, we found friendship, love, community—a third place."[22]

third place *n.* ~ an informal, public gathering place

Welcome to Third Place Brewing

Third Place Brewing in Wichita, Kansas. *Author's collection.*

Tom is a practicing ear surgeon, while his partner, Jason Algya, is a production flight test pilot for Cessna. The two started brewing together close to seventeen years ago. As with all good homebrewers, on brew days, Jason's garage quickly transformed into a destination for friends and family. The passion that the two have shared through the years morphed into the idea of opening a brewery. All their arduous work came to fruition when they opened the doors in 2015. They had to be resourceful, creating the bar out of walnut they found in the basement and building their entire brew system from the ground up.

I keep coming back to Third Place fitting the bill of a classic English pub. The vibe, the space and the beer all are stylistically on point. Keep in mind that Tom started homebrewing back in the 1980s, when he was going through his surgical residency. Over the years, he has honed his brewing talent and is proud to brew to style delivering eight beers precisely to the classic expectations. The clientele that the team serves at Third Place knows what to expect and counts on a strong group of flagship beers complemented by seasonal styles.

Tom has brewed purpose-driven styles motivated by requests from supporters or the need to honor important people in the community. Corvus, a black lager, is a brew that he created for the tanker pilots at the air refueling wing in Wichita. Their squadron name is the Ravens, which inspired the lager's name. Shep's is named after a well-known local soccer coach, paying homage to a man who helped influence Tom's three daughters in their younger years.

Count on a small-scale and intimate experience at Third Place. Tom shared a story about one of his daughter's points of view about the brewery experience. She is a firm believer that beer is meant to be drunk in pints— that the true beer fan is serious about the approach. Bottom line, expect a wonderful experience at Third Place and know that committing to a relationship with one of his sixteen-ounce styles will not lead you astray.

8. HOPPING GNOME BREWING COMPANY

1710 East Douglas Avenue * Wichita, Kansas 67214
316-771-2110
www.hoppinggnome.com/#home
www.facebook.com/HoppingGnome
Brewing System: 5BBL

Gnomes like to drink. They like to drink beer in small doses, but when it comes to a good ale, they love the aromatics of a good IPA, brown or amber. Gnomes also like to hang out with Stacy and Torrey Lattin at their impressive taproom. Gnomies occupy the barstools, bringing their club mugs from home, ready for the first pint to hit the stoneware bottom. Conversations start up immediately in a place that is a welcoming destination, reminiscent of Cheers, a place where everybody knows your name.

Stacy and Torrey love brewing award-winning craft beer and have created the taproom environment where you can come as you are. They aimed for a small and cozy destination, and on opening weekend, they had people lined up for their first pint. The team poured so much beer that they had only two styles left to serve the following weekend.

The couple was inspired by small breweries and tasting rooms in Colorado. Torrey was brewing great beer at home, winning a gold medal for his ESB (extra special bitter), served today at the Gnome. They loved the Jagged Mountain Brewery environment and experience as they watched students studying and families playing board games, while many were enjoying the beer. Eventually, they both left successful careers, with Torrey stepping away from CAD engineering and Stacy leaving her nonprofit work.

Rest assured that as Torrey creates the beer magic with his five-barrel system, Stacy continues to focus on bringing organizations, causes and people together to make Wichita a better place. She

Stacy and Torrey Lattin taking a break at their brewery, Hopping Gnome. *Courtesy of Jessica Noelle Photography.*

Taproom at "the Gnome"—Hopping Gnome Brewing Company in Wichita, Kansas. *Courtesy of Stacy Lattin.*

has worked to partner with other breweries, their business neighbors and nonprofits since the day they opened more than six years ago.

At first, it was not an easy road to travel. They worked with family, friends and a significant Kickstarter fundraiser to make the Hopping Gnome Brewing Company feasible. From the start, the outpouring of support has translated into loyal followers who pack their taproom and small outdoor patio, asking when they will get a bigger space.

Bottom line, this duo has opened a unique brewery that complements the balance of the strong brewery culture in Wichita. They are a classic neighborhood taproom brewery, as is Central Standard Brewing, which is just a short walk from the Gnome. There is magic happening in this brewery. Customers shortened the name of the brewery to "the Gnome" over time, creating a cool handle for this destination, which Stacy and Torrey have gladly adopted.

Torrey has a handful of classic styles, ranging from the Sepia Amber that won a GABF silver medal in 2018 to his Earl ESB and ICT IPA. I was fortunate to visit during the run of their Winter Wheat, a well-balanced black wheat beer brewed using Kansas-grown midnight wheat. He surrounds these popular styles with seasonal rotations, typically resulting in twelve taps for you to select from.

Count on spending a few hours at the Hopping Gnome enjoying the camaraderie, the beer and the spirit created by Stacy, Torrey and the army of gnomes protecting the brewery. Stick with these two in the next few years. I think the duo will have exciting surprises for Gnome fans. All gnomes, who I'm told love ales, are quick to quote Shakespeare: "The best beer is where priests go to drink. For a quart of ale is a dish for a king."[23]

9. CENTRAL STANDARD BREWING

156 South Greenwood * Wichita, Kansas 67211
316-260-8515
www.centralstandardbrewing.com
www.facebook.com/centralstandardbrewing
Brewing System: 7BBL

I had the opportunity to come back to the Central Standard on Wizard Wednesday in early December 2021. I had met with the team earlier in the day prior to their opening and knew that I could not write their profile until I immersed myself in the crowd and felt the good tidings.

If you love dogs and green space, are open to making new friends and have a thirst for exceptional beer, then go hang out at Central Standard Brewing. CSB is in a residential neighborhood with a park across the street. Check out the unique and eclectic metal artwork positioned throughout the brewery created by the artist M.T. Liggett.[24] Ian and Sumer befriended M.T. and proudly display his work created from road signs, car parts, farm equipment and other unique metal remnants. Next time you are on Highway 154

Grab a pint and enjoy the patio at Central Standard Brewing. *Courtesy of Central Standard Brewing, Wichita, Kansas.*

driving west of his hometown toward the Colorado border, keep your eyes open for the legendary Liggett folk art off in the rolling fields.

The team started its craft beer journey more than a decade ago. Ian Crane (co-founder and head brewer) and Andy Boyd (co-founder and operations) started brewing in college. Years later, they decided to highlight their homebrews with their first planned pig roast party. By that point, Nathan Jackal had become part of the brewing team, now partner and brewer at CSB. The team (also including Sumer Crane and Emily Boyd) did not let a Kansas blizzard deter them. In fact, they served four beers using their now defunct beer label, Dank Brewing, to one hundred people. The attendees loved their beer. That feedback gave them confidence to start fermenting their plans to open a brewery.

CSB put Wichita on the craft beer map in its first year, bringing the first GABF medal to the city and brewing community. The old-world French Belgian–style farmhouse ale has been honored twice now for its styling, flavors and effort to pay homage to old-school brewing techniques.

I had an important discussion about the pandemic with this team that was representative of the impact felt by all breweries across the state. Sumer talked about the trauma each of them still copes with that resulted from the six-month shutdown. They all questioned how they were going to come out of the pandemic. Sumer mentioned how hard it was to stomach the evolving challenges to their business, which was exclusively dependent on taproom patronage. CSB is one example of how the brewery community has dealt with the challenges over the last two years. The shifts and pivots, such as investing in a canning line, have made the CSB team stronger.

What started back in the day with Ian and Andy brewing pale ales and wild pitch brits has now become more meaningful, as they give back by supporting their local homebrewing community. They have regulars who will bring in their latest brews for feedback from the trio of brewers. The willingness to share and collaborate kicked off for the trio at Defiance Brewing and came full circle as they helped Larry Cook brew his first beer for the thirsty crowd at Dodge City Brewing.

Step up to the bar like I did at CSB and enjoy the environment. You will see folks who met at the bar on a night like Bluegrass Tuesday or Wizard Wednesday who have since become good friends. Ian loves what they have created with their community. Central Standard's steady influx of new beer styles will draw you in. Check out its thirteen styles on tap and hang out in a 1970s living room curated by Sumer. Enjoy!

10. WICHITA BREWING COMPANY

West Wichita Brewpub * 8815 West 13th Street, Suite 100 *
  Wichita, Kansas 67212
316-440-2885
East Wichita Brewpub * 535 North Woodlawn Street *
  Wichita, Kansas 67208
316-440-4885
www.wichitabrew.com
www.facebook.com/Wichitabrew
Brewing System: 20BBL

The Wichita brewing community rejoiced when the Great American Beer Festival (GABF) judges announced that Wichita Brewing Company had won a gold medal. The medal came in the "Old Ale or Strong Ale or Barley Wine" category, for its barley wine called Chris Barley in a Little Coat. Cody Sherwood, head brewer, told me, "It could be easy for judges to get lost in the booze or complexity of barley wine, so to win gold was unbelievable."[25]

The craft beer fans who frequent the broad selection of Wichita breweries are rejoicing as well. The gold secured by Wichita Brewing (WBC) is its

Chris Barley in a Little Coat barleywine, Gold Medal, 2021 GABF. *Courtesy of Wichita Brewing Company, Wichita, Kansas.*

second GABF medal[26] thus far. In 2017, it won a silver medal for Shaven Yak, an English-style brown ale.[27] Still, the brew team at WBC did not rest on its laurels. It took the Shaven Yak to the World Beer Cup in 2018 and brought home a gold![28] Two of its Wichita brewery friends have won as well. Central Standard Brewing won two gold GABF medals in back-to-back years, most recently in 2019, for its Standard Issue Belgian Saison. Do not forget the gnomes at Hopping Gnome. Torrey brought home their first GABF medal in 2018, a silver for their Sepia Amber.

Great beer is being brewed and enjoyed in Wichita. The brewing community no doubt has spent evenings together celebrating as a group, knowing that the stronger they are, the more compelling it is for us to travel to Wichita to check out the beer scene.

Jeremy Horn (co-owner of WBC) and Cody kicked off a new podcast back in July 2021 called *Under the Lid*, which has elevated the beer culture within the region through the edgy, cool behind-the-scenes discussions that often involve sideways conversations and drinking—but not necessarily in that order! The two behind this successful series posted their forty-fourth episode right before I submitted this manuscript.

WBC, founded by Jeremy Horn and his homebrewing friend Greg Gifford, opened its west brewpub location in 2011. Jeremy said that the two share a "light switch" personality. When the switch is flipped on, as it was in 2009, the two are 100 percent vested in making things happen. Wichita Brewing Company has been on a strong ten-year trajectory, opening an east side brewpub to capture an audience who wanted WBC in their backyard, followed by the opening of its large production operation and event space.

How did the two and their team arrive at this spot in early 2022? It started with the grass-roots efforts of Jeremy, serving up popular homebrews, complemented by the pizza that Greg started pulling out of his wood-fired oven in his backyard. Successful beer and pizza recipes led to taking the professional leap. Two of their beer styles have won medals in the last ten years and can be found next to six great house brew taps.

Cody came to WBC after four years of brewing at Lb. Brewing Company in Hays. He told me, "I don't really love a specific role as head brewer. I just fuckin' absolutely love, adore and cherish every day that I wake up, and I get to produce beer and every two weeks they put money into my account."[29]

Cody produced the idea for *Under the Lid* and is happy that he and Jeremy have hit every goal on the podcast, not losing sight of how it serves as an information hub for the backstories of brewers, authors and chefs, while elevating the hilarity of random nonsense. Cody and the team keep rotating in seasonal favorites, while also stretching our tastes with the "Mad Scientist Experimental Series." Beer fans cannot get bored or say that they cannot find a beer to their liking as they look down murderers' row at seventeen tap handles.

When I met with Jeremy and Cody to talk shop, learn about WBC and be a guest on their podcast, I was struck by Jeremy's intensity and commitment, which was balanced by Cody's understated and irreverent personality. Perhaps the two had me fooled nevertheless, as I walked out of their production space impressed with their vision. Through the scale of their business and their passion for innovation, squeezing every moment of life out of each minute in a day, success will pave the future path.

That same passion shines through with events that light up their social media. In March 2022, the team celebrated, hosting the sixth annual Wichita Brewing Relay Marathon, the course stretching between their two brewpubs. The marathon event is a celebration of life, exercise, beer and happiness. Another event managed by Cody in 2022, which will reach those suffering from mental health issues, is the first annual "Beer Fest." Wichita Brewing Company has partnered with all Wichita breweries and some of the best breweries across the Midwest to raise money for mental health clinics in the Wichita area.

The joy that Cody expressed to me about winning the gold medal in 2021 is evident in the work the entire team at Wichita Brewing Company does to make our experiences unforgettable, thanks to great pizza, award-winning beer and a casual, comfortable brewpub vibe. WBC is a winner!

11. RIVER CITY BREWING COMPANY

150 North Mosley * Wichita, Kansas 67202
316-263-2739
rivercitybrewingco.com
www.facebook.com/RiverCityBrewingICT
Brewing System: 7BBL

A definition of history is that of a continuous, chronological record of major events of a particular institution. Breweries in Kansas are an institution, and River City Brewing Company's opening is an important event worth celebrating. First came Lawrence's Free State Brewing Company in 1989, followed by River City four years later. River City was groundbreaking in Wichita, standing alone as the only craft brewery for eight years until Wichita Brewing Company opened in 2011. Chris Arnold, owner of River City, said, "I didn't know how lonely we were until WBC opened."[30] The sense of community took hold immediately, as the two breweries helped each other, cheered each other on and drank together after work.

I walked into River City Brewing Company on an unusual sixty-degree January day under a Kansas blue sky, buffeted by strong southwestern winds. The building has stood on this corner since 1909 and has been home to many businesses. Its history began as a paint company, later transitioning from a grocery store to a hide company, appropriate considering the history

Cheers at River City
Brewing Company.
*Courtesy of River City
Brewing Company, Wichita,
Kansas.*

of Wichita. The old bones speak to you in the brewpub environment, with exposed brick walls and thunderous timber beams overlooking the tables, bar and brewhouse.

River City has had a strong history of talented head brewers. Dan Norton of Nortons Brewing Company developed his brewing skills at River City, mentoring others such as Logan Carter, who has moved to Charlotte, North Carolina, as part of a team opening a new brewery. For the last three years, Brandon Fairs has been walking in the footsteps of his predecessors. The sixteen taps that pour daily start with a group of flagship styles that cater to most patrons' preferences. The Tornado Alley IPA is a top seller, as is the Harvester Wheat.

Brandon talked to me about their extensive barrel aging program, mentioning that they are known for the barrel-aged stout series. He also shared breaking news for 2022, starting with the addition of a side tap that will highlight a slow-pour pilsner. A new brewhouse system will be installed in early summer of 2022, which Brandon is excited about, knowing that style consistency will improve and efficiencies in the brewing process will give him and his co-brewer time to utilize elsewhere.

Brandon is a people person who enjoys those moments where he can talk with patrons and work to build bridges to new craft beer styles based on their preferences. He loves when someone comes in and mentions that they do not like IPAs. "IPAs are like coffee. You don't like it until you start drinking it,"[31] he said. Brandon is enthusiastic when talking about his beer, breaking down barriers and creating new experiences for his brewery community.

Communities are central to our Kansas breweries. Chris and his team at River City do their best to deliver great experiences to new and old customers alike. That shared motivation is a link that brings the brewery teams together often to celebrate, commiserate, deliberate, educate and have a pint or three. Chris captured the magic behind the brewery community in Wichita, which is the most vibrant one in the state, saying, "This town is really cool. We all talk and work together in a variety of ways. It is fun when we all hang out and drink each other's beer."[32]

12. HANK IS WISER BREWERY

213 North Main Street * Cheney, Kansas 67025
316-542-0113
www.facebook.com/hankiswiserbrewery
Brewing System: ½BBL

April 1 can be a memorable day for both the giver and recipient of tricks, surprises and laugh-out-loud moments. The day back in 2005 carries great significance for the Sanford family. On that day, not only did Hank Sanford, founder and owner of Hank Is Wiser Brewery, retire after a storied sales career, but he also determined that it was a momentous day to open a brewery in Cheney.[33]

Hank, Jane and their son, Steve, enjoy a good sense of humor. Back in Hank's homebrewing days, the label he used for his brews was Hankweiser. Hank, who has spent close to half a century building an extensive collection of older Anheuser-Busch memorabilia, is a Budweiser fan. Steve described how his dad landed with the name of the brewery: Hank decided that the name Hank Is Wiser would be the closest that he could go in paying honor to the giant of American breweries.

Steve mentioned to Kevin, my in-law, friend and faithful companion on many brewery treks, that "we always say, Hank is 'Hank,' my mom is the 'wiser,' and I am the little 'is.'"[34]

Steve has taken over the operations of the brewery as his dad stepped away. He and his mom, Jane, are at the helm of the brewery as the family gets up and running again. Not only is Hank Is Wiser fueled by the smallest brewhouse in the state, but it also shut down for eighteen months from the outset of the pandemic until late summer 2021. The closure was the longest duration of any breweries in the state. The Sanfords took their family and their community's health to heart when they made the tough decision.

Steve, who started his brewing career as an assistant brewer for Dan Norton at River City in Wichita, is getting back into the saddle in Cheney. The day of our visit, Steve was busy getting four fruited beers on tap in anticipation of their Friday and Saturday weekly

Hank Is Wiser Brewery in Cheney. *Courtesy of Hank Is Wiser Brewery in Cheney, Kansas.*

hours. The community that supports the brewery has come back with a thirst, which has made it challenging for Steve to get ahead of beer production.

The people who collect at Hank Is Wiser are there for the barbecue and the beer. The building, built in 1898 and originally home to a mercantile store, offers patrons long tables reminiscent of German beer halls. Come to Cheney and expect to leave with new friends, satiated on conversations, ribs prepared by Steve and a pint or two.

The brewery has unique features that have put Hank's on the map as a destination. For the first time in eighteen months, Steve hosted a monthly Cheney Beer Club gathering. For twenty dollars, one can come in for an evening, ready to enjoy four slices of pizza, seven tasters of beer from around the country and a healthy pint of Hank's. Steve mentioned that they historically have drawn more than one hundred people to these monthly events.

While visiting with Steve, we were introduced to their collection of Utopias from Samuel Adams Brewery in Boston. The Sanfords have the only collection of Utopias, an extreme barrel-aged beer across the brewery community in Kansas. The releases are limited-edition runs that can knock your socks off, as the rich aroma and flavors of a 28 percent ABV beer are slowly enjoyed. We tasted an ounce of two vintages, 2009 and 2019 Utopias, walking away fully on board with how revolutionary an experience imbibing in Utopias can be.

Several times, I have looked at a Facebook post from June 11, 2021, announcing that they were not fully reopened but had some wisdom to spread at Hanks, which has always been an expectation for their fans. Steve talked about how great their patrons are. Everybody comes in to just have an enjoyable time at what is the old-school, original Kansas small-town brewery. Those new taprooms that are opening in rural towns from Council Grove to Courtland need to give a nod to the originals that helped pave the way for the new old-school brewery owners and brewers.

The Sanfords have turned the lights on for seventeen years on Main Street in Cheney. Steve brought it all home, simply saying, "We are just here for the beer."[35]

13. LADYBIRD BREWING

523 Main * Winfield, Kansas 67516
620-222-7558
https://www.ladybird.beer
www.facebook.com/ladybirdbrewing
Brewing System: 3BBL

The garage door is pushed open by two talented, enthusiastic women who will help you connect, celebrate great beer and make memories at Ladybird Brewing. Step up to the bar, strike up a conversation with the team and toast friends, family and new acquaintances on the patio over a pint. The old bones of the brewery were home to a filling station and garage from the mid-1950s until Kaydee and Laura's dream moved closer to reality with the purchase of the building in 2019. The transformation of the space from the days of exhaust-stained walls and layers of dirt on the floors is remarkable. You will find an openness as you grab a bar stool at their L-shaped bar and contemplate what your first pint will be.

The community of Winfield is Kaydee and Laura Riggs-Johnson's home. Friends and fans from the four corners of Winfield used to stop by several times an evening while the two perched at the top of scaffolding, painting the ceiling. The conversations ranged from jokingly asking for crowlers to

Visiting Kaydee and Laura at Ladybird Brewing. *Courtesy of Ladybird Brewing, Winfield, Kansas.*

words of encouragement in advance of their opening. Their dream was tested by the pandemic. As they grappled with equipment delays, their focus on the positives on this journey is remarkable. "It is gonna happen," Kaydee said, followed by, "I know it, I can see it, I can feel it."[36] As one carful of supporters stopped to ask about the progress, Kaydee made sure to call out as they left, "Stay thirsty!"

As a young adult, Kaydee watched her parents occasionally drain a Coors or Keystone Light after a long day of work. That was all she knew beer to be until her awakening in college, when she tasted Major Tom's Pomegranate Wheat beer from Fort Collins Brewery. "It sort of blew my mind,"[37] Kaydee said. Although she was not of age to raise a pint on this trip, Kaydee was mesmerized by sitting in the great brewery spaces. Her newfound fascination in craft beer and the brewery experience while visiting the Fort Collins, Odell and New Belgium breweries were the catalyst for a future in the craft beer industry.

Laura found her way to this shared path with Kaydee in life and all things beer through her role at a winery, diving into the fermentation processes and the science of developing a quality bottle of wine. The idea of owning a brewery remained alive for Laura, who has proven repeatedly that she excels at taking on new challenges, from playing the guitar to winning CrossFit competitions to becoming a lawyer. The two started homebrewing just before they celebrated their marriage five years ago. Since then, they stepped up to a scaled-down commercial brewing system. Thanks to the strength of Laura's brewhouse process management and Kaydee's passion for cellaring and experimenting with recipes, their beer will not disappoint.

Today, their biggest stressor is finding the time to brew more beer to keep up with the community's thirst! As Kaydee said, "We are grateful to have good problems."[38]

What styles can you find on tap? Expect balance and flavor, with styles ranging from brown to blonde ales, West Coast IPAs, saisons and crazy, juicy, hazy IPAs. They like to put a twist on flagship styles to keep you coming back. Expect to see a changing landscape of food trucks and a Ladybird bike motoring down Winfield's Main Street to pick up orders at the classic Burger Station. Find comfort in knowing that the moment you enter the brewery, you have immediate friends in Kaydee and Laura. Pause for a moment while enjoying the space and toast these brewers.

In a 2019 national study, the number of female brewers had grown to 7.5 percent of all brewers.[39] Statistics reflect that in the U.S. craft beer industry, women are significantly underrepresented. Growth of women in our state brewer population is on pace with national levels. Our state craft beer community should set a goal to exceed national growth. I hope that talented brewers such as Kaydee and Laura will inspire and mentor women in the Kansas homebrewing community who dream of taking the next step. Diversity within our brewer community will continue to create variety, flavor, innovation and discovery for craft beer fans.

Chapter 3

GETTING HOPPY WITH FREE STATE AND YAKIMANIAC

I n my mind, you are never a master of this craft,"[1] said Geoff Deman, head brewer at Free State Brewing Company in Lawrence. He went on to say, "There is always something to learn. It could be learning about new techniques and innovation. Every year, there is new research and renewed interest in historical styles."[2] In Geoff's two decades in the brewing industry, the number of breweries has grown from one thousand to more than nine thousand in the United States.[3] The industry has been changing dramatically, not only witnessed through the growth in the number of breweries in our country but also highlighted by the style trends and innovative techniques in the brewing process.

I had the good fortune to sit with Geoff weeks after his annual Yakima Valley hop selection trip. Geoff reminisced with me about his eight years of professional brewing in Seattle prior to moving back to his hometown of Lawrence in 2002 to brew at Free State, the brewery that first exposed him to the possibilities of beer, when he worked as a busser there in its inaugural year. Each hop selection trip to the Pacific Northwest means a stopover for a day or two to his old stomping grounds in Seattle, drawing inspiration and reconnecting with the Seattle beer and food scene that led to his early growth as a brewer. It's a familiar scene, but also one that echoes the exponential growth in craft beer since his time in the Pacific Northwest. Those changes are echoed in Yakima. "It's kind of crazy how much Yakima has changed since my first visit."[4]

Fifteen years ago, Geoff ventured into Yakima Valley for the first time, spending two days in a series of hops seminars. "My allergies went into overdrive" as he arrived in Yakima Valley, a high desert environment that is uniquely suited to growing hops. At that time, there were no breweries in Yakima Valley, which is hard to believe, considering the dominant role the valley played in the hop industry. Today, the valley contains about 75 percent of the hop acreage in the United States,[5] as well as more than a dozen breweries.

As Geoff went on to describe the sensory overload he experienced each year coming into the valley, I could tell that the memories had not diminished since his first trip. "You hit this wall of aroma. Initially it is apples, pears, and orchard fruits." Geoff continued, painting a picture. "As you get closer to the city, you get punched in the face with the aroma of hops—it is intoxicating."[6]

Geoff's responsibilities have grown through the years at Free State, now including making the key yearly hop selections and hop contracting, ensuring that there is ample supply of the hop varieties that populate Free State's flagship brews. Think about the number one flagship beer at Free State. Yakimaniac IPA is a signature beer for the brewery, blending two hops to create the flavors and aromas of tropical fruit in an incredible golden-hued IPA. An inability to procure these unique hop varieties could make for a vastly different brew, one that doesn't read as Yakimaniac. "We have to cover our needs,"[7] Geoff said with emphasis.

This style was inspired by information shared by friend Tom Bastian (now a safety engineer at Dogfish Head in Milton, Delaware) about directions some Philadelphia area breweries were taking with their IPAs, particularly adding substantial amounts of oats to those brews. Deman saw it as a perfect opportunity to incorporate some new techniques in dry hopping being pioneered by some West Coast brewers, marrying those with the Philadelphia takes on the style. "Yakimaniac was spawned by the direction certain brewers were taking," he said. Geoff went on to talk about the innovative approach with this recipe. "I wanted to emphasize more of the tropical characteristics in this one hop through a new process."[8]

The trips to Yakima Valley typically occur late in each year's hop harvest in early fall. Geoff collaborates with his hop brokers on timing of those appointments to ensure that enough of the fields have been harvested to provide a reasonable selection of lots to choose from. The goal is to find the lot that most closely mimics the character of Yakimaniac, thus ensuring continuity of the brand profile. This year presented unique global warming challenges, which he hopes will not become more common, such as the

Getting Hoppy with Free State and Yakimaniac. *Courtesy of Free State Brewing Company, Lawrence, Kansas.*

devastating fires and record-breaking heat waves. These could have long-term consequences for the industry.

As he brewed Yakimaniac for the first time, written on the brew sheet's line for "Beer Type" was the name "IPA Brain," inspired by the pizza joint he enjoyed visiting in Philly with Bastian, called Pizza Brain. As Geoff worked to hit aromatic and style notes that were his goal with this beer, he wandered back into his head, drawing from the scent memories of pulling into Yakima for the first time. This beer had hops on the brain, to be sure, maniacally so.

Free State opened in 1989 and is Kansas's original craft brewery. We have witnessed significant brewery growth in Lawrence in the last five years. In the next chapter, you can read about the eighteen breweries in the area, including the recent additions in Lawrence. Kansas I-70 serves as the main artery on this map, leading you toward Topeka plus seven towns north and south of the interstate on some great state highways.

Free State is elevating beer in the state. Enjoy a Yakimaniac while having memorable conversations and experiences at 636 Massachusetts Street. Make sure to not spill a drop on this book!

#BecauseWithoutBeer…

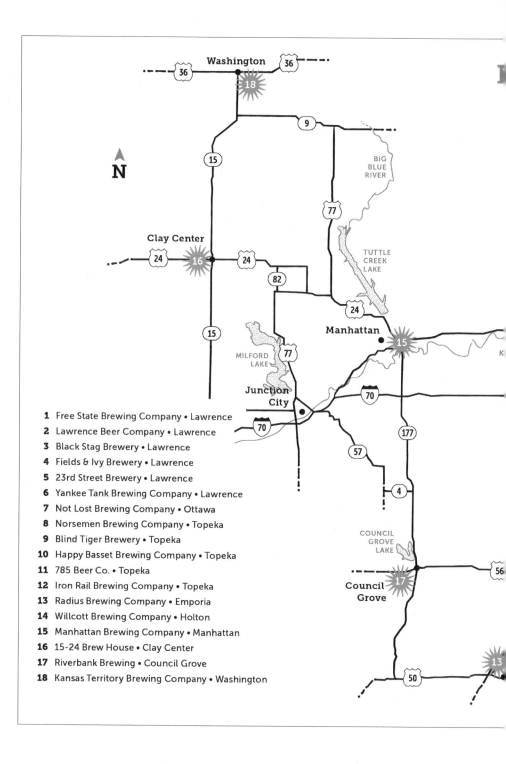

1 Free State Brewing Company • Lawrence
2 Lawrence Beer Company • Lawrence
3 Black Stag Brewery • Lawrence
4 Fields & Ivy Brewery • Lawrence
5 23rd Street Brewery • Lawrence
6 Yankee Tank Brewing Company • Lawrence
7 Not Lost Brewing Company • Ottawa
8 Norsemen Brewing Company • Topeka
9 Blind Tiger Brewery • Topeka
10 Happy Basset Brewing Company • Topeka
11 785 Beer Co. • Topeka
12 Iron Rail Brewing Company • Topeka
13 Radius Brewing Company • Emporia
14 Willcott Brewing Company • Holton
15 Manhattan Brewing Company • Manhattan
16 15-24 Brew House • Clay Center
17 Riverbank Brewing • Council Grove
18 Kansas Territory Brewing Company • Washington

k Chalk to Wildcat Country

Eighteen breweries with Kansas I-70 as the main artery, kicking off with the oldest brew/pub in the state, Free State Brewing Company, and ending with Kansas Territory Brewing Company, which has the largest brewhouse production capability in the Sunflower State.

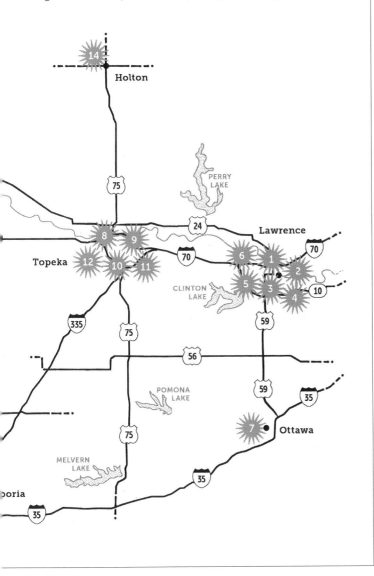

Rock Chalk to Wildcat Country map. *Courtesy of Christy Schneider, Inkello Design & Letterpress, East Lawrence, Kansas.*

Chapter 4

ROCK CHALK TO
WILDCAT COUNTRY

1. FREE STATE BREWING COMPANY

636 Massachusetts Street * Lawrence, Kansas 66044
785-843-4555
www.freestatebrewing.com
www.facebook.com/freestatebrewing
Brewing System: 14BBL

Free State and my family are deeply connected. It starts with the monthly visits my wife, Ivy, and I have made to the brewery over fifteen years, approaching 175 by the end of 2022. Why are we so drawn to 636 Massachusetts Street? The vibrancy of downtown, the patio abuzz with friends, the happy noise wafting over us as we walk in for another meal and several pints of great beer are our definitive answer. We are comfortable, happy, connected and feel like we are part of a family.

Speaking of family, our youngest daughter, Meaghan, had her first date with her future husband, Chris Orlando, at Free State. The great news for us is that the two decided to get married, bringing two grandchildren into our world in the last three years. On their wedding day, they celebrated a sense of belonging to Free State, stopping with their photographer to capture images of the two on the patio, where it all started for them.

As Geoff Deman, head brewer at Free State, started his life journey after high school, he fell headfirst into homebrewing, getting introduced to it while spending time with friends who were attending Berkeley. He returned to Lawrence, bringing his newfound passion and equipment with him. He remembers that summer, how rewarding it was as he brewed five-gallon styles weekly, which elevated his appreciation and love for the process and ingredients involved. Geoff found himself heading west again, this time destined for Seattle. His professional brewery upbringing started while there. He developed his professional skills, wearing many hats for Pyramid Brewing Company and Pike Brewing Company.

After deciding to return to Lawrence, good fortune came his way after a six-pack of Pike Brewing beer and his résumé were left by a friend at the host station at Free State, finding their way into the right hands. Steve Bradt, former head of brewing, liked what he saw and drank, quickly offering Geoff a brewery job. The rest is history. Geoff thinks of himself as the creative director in charge of a significant operation today. The brewpub is his home most days, with the brewhouse serving as his research and development arm of the business.

The production facility in East Lawrence brews the flagship beer styles and takes on the distribution volume that must be fed. This has allowed him to shift the brewing focus at the brewpub to new styles, which are introduced

Patio shot at 636 Massachusetts Street, home of Free State Brewing Company, Lawrence, Kansas. *Author's collection.*

on the beer board frequently. The new releases find their way on the board, complementing the renowned flagship styles that keep up to eighteen taps busy at the bar.

Geoff Evans told me that a goal at the brewery was to "take the public aspect of pub and have community within these stone walls."[1] Through the years, the stone walls have warmly welcomed their faithful, fueling lively conversations and memorable experiences, such as a first date resulting in a wedding and life together. The brewery has been fortunate, offering quality beer due to the efforts of two head brewers and their teams over the last thirty years. Geoff, who succeeded Steve Bradt, the original head of brewing, has carried the torch of success forward.

"We make great beer here,"[2] Geoff noted. What drives Geoff is the curiosity in brewing, which motivates his thirst to constantly learn. He coaches his brew team to have their customers in mind with anything they do. The goal for Geoff is simple: "We want to make sure that everybody has something that they are happy with." He went on to emphasize, "I am constantly learning, I am constantly looking through my peers, through reading, through the internet to enhance my education regarding beer and brewing."[3]

Geoff often finds himself enjoying a pint with friends and fans of the brewery on the patio as another day slips by, with the sun setting over downtown. He reflected for a moment, telling me, "It is very satisfying when you feel like you have done well. When people come back to you with praise, that is what it is all about, making people happy."[4]

Step into the warm, boisterous Free State environment, knowing that the following quote, important to the brewery, captures the significance of spending time with friends, enjoying camaraderie and peace: "Because without beer, things do not seem to go as well."

2. LAWRENCE BEER COMPANY

826 Pennsylvania Street * Lawrence, Kansas 66044
785-856-0453
4811 Bob Billings Parkway * Lawrence, Kansas 66049
785-856-0596
www.lawrencebeerco.com
www.facebook.com/lawrencebeercowest
Brewing System: 15BBL

Bring your dog. Down the street. Up the alley. Lawrence Beer Company, Lawrence, Kansas. *Author's collection.*

Matt Williams, owner of Lawrence Beer Company, knew that his brewery was destined for 826 Pennsylvania Street in the Warehouse Arts District in East Lawrence. The one-hundred-year-old Seedco building spoke to him, knowing that Lawrence Beer Company would become a vital gathering place for its neighbors and local community. As a longstanding patron of LBC, I can speak from experience that the vibe is awesome. I have spent many nights with my wife, Ivy, on the outside patio, watching the neighborhood migrate down the street to the brewery, couples, dogs and strollers galore.

LBC has started to extend its reach in Lawrence, introducing its first neighborhood location on the west side of town. Matt talked to me about the brewing industry and how the days of national breweries opening like Boulevard are over. We are witnessing this movement in our state with new breweries opening in small towns, with a focus on serving their communities. Matt told me, "Our expansion will be more like what we did in West Lawrence. We would transfer our concept to a different neighborhood."[5]

Central to the success at LBC is its head brewer, Sam McClain, who became part of the team as the brewery was brought to life. Sam designed the glycol system and mapped out the brewhouse layout; he was also known to have a hammer in hand, standing next to Matt, putting up interior walls. Sam's homebrewing days started out of necessity while in college in Chicago. He could not afford to buy beer, so the brewing journey began. His professional brewing experience scaled up quickly during his days at Half Acre Beer Company in Chicago, driven by the brewery's dramatic six-year growth. Sam focused heavily on the processes of brewing and took a broad skill set to Boulevard in Kansas City, where he worked with filtration and brewing.

Sam shared that he has "a dream brewing scenario." LBC is focused on serving its community and neighborhood great beer. "I can brew whatever we want whenever we want to make it," he said. Distribution is not part of their business plan, which Sam followed by saying, "So we don't have to fit into the hype machine of national brewing."[6] Sam described his brewing approach visually with two circles. The first circle is focused on brewing clean, hop-forward, modern IPAs and pale ales. The second circle is home to brewing traditional beers with elevated flavors. "I select an ingredient to focus on to create a beautiful melding of elevated flavors that are ramped up a little bit,"[7] Sam said. He loves session IPAs and pale ales, which play a dominant role within the tap selection of up to twelve styles.

I was encouraged to learn from Sam that the Lawrence brewers are collaborative, using group texting as the platform for the community to share resources, ask for help and talk about the potential of future collaborations. The pandemic has slowed down the timeline to make things happen. "It has been on our radar for a while," Matt said, concluding, "It's in the future."[8]

Matt and Sam are authentic leaders and are committed to looking at everything they do with a long-term view. What matters to them is that their energy is focused on creating connections in the community, serving them, pouring pints, while also pouring their passion and creativity into cause-driven support. Matt wrapped up, saying, "What we do is have a large voice, large space and beer and food that people really like."

3. BLACK STAG BREWERY

623 Massachusetts Street * Lawrence, Kansas 66044
785-766-1163
blackstagbrew.com
www.facebook.com/BlackStagBrewery
Brewing System: 10BBL

Tasters on the patio at Black Stag Brewery in Lawrence, Kansas, with my daughter Meaghan and granddaughter, Luna. *Author's collection.*

"Beer is to be shared,"[9] Kathryn Myers said as we settled in for our conversation. She and her husband, John, are partners, along with Kathryn's dad, Bill, of Black Stag Brewery. The couple decided to chase their dream after John's homebrewing created a following of fans, resulting in frequent driveway and KU football tailgating parties. Opening Black Stag in February 2019 was destined to happen because of the brewing history in John's family, with Hampton ancestors in South Carolina brewing in the late 1800s.

My daughter Meaghan and granddaughter, Luna, joined me and Kathryn on the patio for an enjoyable hour-long conversation. Kathryn told us how she challenged her dad, Bill, saying, "This is your fault. If you had not bought the Mr. Beer Kit for John, this never would have happened!"[10] John gravitated to homebrewing, finding that his biochemistry education and background accelerated his grasp of the brewing process. His thirst for learning led him to taking Siebel Institute classes to further his understanding of the brewing processes and management of a brewhouse.

Today, as head brewer, John has established a strong lineup of twelve styles that are grounded in traditional recipes. When possible, the brew team will use ingredients sourced from the country of origin for the specific style. The beer lineup starts with easy-drinking ales and lagers and finishes with a great lineup of malty styles. My granddaughter, Luna, continued to sleep as the conversation shifted to all things KU, with Kathryn, John, Meaghan and her husband all Jayhawk alumni. Black Stag celebrates their loyalty and love for KU, with their flagship 1865 black lager, named for the year that KU became a university.

"Mizzou can go to hell,"[11] Kathryn declared with a smile. She went on to talk about the blood, sweat and tears that she and John have expended since construction started in 2018. Today, Kathryn is all things front of the house, as well as managing the restaurant side of the business. Her twenty-seven years as a practicing attorney, in combination with an MBA, provided her the moxie to make things work in a world that was brand new to her.

61

The history at 623 Massachusetts goes back to the early 1800s. The original building served as a warehouse, storing goods that barges delivered on the Kansas River. Today, the brewery has a basement event space. The couple has plans to grow, including the possibility of taking full ownership of the building, with the goal to build out a second-floor space that could host weddings. History shines on the second floor, with lofty ceilings supported by tresses that came from a now defunct river bridge crossing.

Luna, a six-month-old brewery fan at the time, stirred late in our conversation as we ordered our pints and dinner. Kathryn believes that Lawrence has room for a few more breweries and its first distillery. She would love to see the city become a craft beer destination, similar on a smaller scale to a Fort Collins, Colorado environment. Collaboration and a tight brewing community are lacking in Lawrence when I compare the scene to the Wichita Way. Beer fans will flock to Lawrence fueled by an energy and collaborative passion if the brewing community decides to join hands united.

"Hi, sweetheart, how are you?" Kathryn softly said to Luna as our conversation ended. Meaghan and I sat back and digested the conversation we had just had while enjoying our beer and food. The Black Stag team's commitment, that no matter what your favorite brew is, it will have a cold one ready that will make you happy and keep you coming back, rings true. Next time you are in Lawrence to do a brewery crawl, make sure to include Black Stag.

4. FIELDS & IVY BREWERY

706 East 23rd Street * Lawrence, Kansas 66046
785-274-8429
fieldsandivy.com
www.facebook.com/FieldsAndIvy
Brewing System: 20BBL

Expect to feel like you are part of the family when visiting Fields & Ivy Brewery. Owners Cory and Veronica Johnston have created a brewery that centers on a talented work family focused on delivering great food and beer to their community of supporters. Cory started homebrewing while living in Atlanta and working in the financial sector. He dreamed of opening a brewery someday, while he and Veronica continued to work in their fields.

Cory Johnston, owner of Fields & Ivy Brewery, welcoming you to his Lawrence, Kansas brewery. *Courtesy of Michael Taylor, Lawrence, Kansas.*

Cory merged two interests, homebrewing and agriculture, initially through raising the roof on their family farm in Wellsville, Kansas. A dream that had lain dormant for years came to life as Cory pursued the art and science needed to turn mother earth's bounty into a compelling beer.

Kansas is one of the top grain-growing regions in the world.[12] Cory and the team have started to take advantage of high-quality grains such as his farm-grown barley used in the Kansas Lager, farm-grown wheat used in the Summer Pasture American wheat and authentic heirloom Silver Mine corn (developed by Ernest W. Young in 1907 in Lawrence) used in their flagship Worboys American Lager. Stop by to be part of the brewery community, while enjoying a relaxing afternoon in their beer garden, celebrating its connection to Kansas agriculture with a pint.

Dan Chivetta and Connor Stefanik, the brew team, consistently offer a strong selection of styles. At the same time, they love to experiment with new techniques or ingredients, using oak barrels for small-batch brews. Dan, head brewer, has a strong brewing background that continues to translate into authentic flavor and excellent quality.

Dan, who was within reach of getting his English degree, walked away to pursue either culinary or brewing school. Thankfully for us, he took the brewing path, reading any brewing book within reach. Siebel Institute[13] and its brewing certification program opened doors to start his career. Dan brings that crazy combination of proudly being a beer dork with an encyclopedic knowledge that has grown through his years brewing in Chicago and with Boulevard in KC.

Chivetta has come a long way from his first year of brewing when he realized, "I had no idea what I was doing."[14] His decade at Boulevard working for his brewmaster mentor Steve Pauwels built a skill set that encompassed all facets of brewing. Today, Dan comfortably knows the "process like the back of his hand." He is having fun again, working with state-of-the-art equipment in what he believes to be the nicest brewhouse in the KC area. "This thing," Dan said with a smile, "is a Ferrari."[15]

5. 23ᴿᴰ STREET BREWERY

3512 Clinton Parkway * Lawrence, Kansas 66047
785-856-2337
www.brew23.com
www.facebook.com/brew23
Brewing System: 15BBL

Walk into 23rd Street Brewery and immediately get wrapped up in KU Jayhawk colors and memorabilia in this brewpub. Look upward and notice that this is one of two breweries in the state of Kansas that has a brewhouse on a floor above the guests. Look around at the multiple big-screen TVs, displaying local and regional sports. The brewery has a youthful vibe to it, while still catering to all ages. Matt Llewellyn, owner of 23rd Street since 2004, is the leader behind the renaming of the brewpub, as well as the introduction of meals linked to local celebrities, such as the Bill Self Mac & Cheese.

This locally owned brewpub on the west side of Lawrence has a fifteen-barrel brewhouse that is situated in some of the tightest brewery space I have seen across the Sunflower State. The brewer, Chad Royer, had to dance around my in-law, Kevin, and me as we checked out the vessels, cooler and grain rooms. Chad is the fourth brewer in the history of 23rd Street. Matt needed Chad to fill an unexpected void created by the departure of the last brewer. The spirit of the brewing community held strong as two former head brewers at 23rd Street spent days brewing alongside Chad.

Chad feels the pressure to deliver flagship beers with consistency to a customer base that has supported Matt and team at 23rd Street for close to two decades. The previous brewer had established a style balance, which keeps the flagships pouring, while exploring the beer style trends such as hazy IPAs. Expect Chad to continue on that course, while introducing new styles such as a milk stout that he can play with, introducing a rotation of flavors.

Second-story brewhouse at 23rd Street Brewery in Lawrence, Kansas. *Author's collection.*

The power of community is central to Matt's focus in his role as owner at the brewpub. He had the opportunity to buy the building several years after taking ownership of the business. He collaborated with wonderful owners Jack and Martha Rose, who were longstanding Lawrence residents. After Jack passed away, Martha wanted Matt to get ownership of the building. Matt told me that he was forever indebted to her because of how instrumental she was in making it happen.

I am impressed with Matt's approach to his business and brewery family. He told me that through his professional career, he had become a disciple of Ken Blanchard and the management philosophies that Blanchard had shared through his sixty-plus books. Two books, *The One Minute Manager*[16] and *Raving Fans*,[17] have been instrumental in the success of the brewpub and his ability to weather the pandemic. Matt's goal for 23rd Street Brewery is to be known for great beer, food and service. Blanchard and his lessons show up when his waitstaff tries to over-deliver on guest expectations (shout out to Emma, who took an enthusiastic interest in my book), creating an experience worth repeating the next time you visit and hoist a pint of Wave the Wheat!

6. YANKEE TANK BREWING

3520 West 6th Street * Lawrence, Kansas 66046
785-749-2999
www.facebook.com/yankeetankbrewing
Brewing System: 10BBL

This is the only profile in the book that was written without having the richness of an enjoyable conversation with the team about the heartbeat of the brewery. Despite multiple failed attempts to connect, I was able to gather material from a visit I made with my in-law, Kevin, enjoying a light lunch with a flight of four samplers.

Yankee Tank Brewing, established in 2015, has an East Lawrence production facility that churns out beer that you can find on tap at Henry T's locations in Topeka and Lawrence.

Angelo Ruiz, head brewer, had ten-plus years of homebrewing experience prior to becoming part of the Yankee Tank brewing family. Ruiz had an interesting opening act with Yankee Tank. He had posted tough critiques about a Yankee Tank beer on untappd.com. The brewer at the time invited him to visit the production facility to talk further about the style to understand Angelo's point of view. After a lengthy conversation, the brewer, who agreed with Ruiz's thinking, offered him a job in the brewery.

Angelo brings excitement to Yankee Tank through interesting innovations and collaborations that keep the brewery fans engaged. Visit the Henry T's in Lawrence and enjoy a pint while cheering on the Jayhawks in a Big 12 conference hoops game. Ruiz has developed a strong flagship style roster, which he continues to complement with seasonal and innovative brewing, including the launch of the Against the Grain, a gluten-free style. Credit goes to Yankee Tank for having a gluten-free tap handle; it's the only Kansas brewery offering this type of beer.

The naming of this brewery pays homage to Yankee Tank's Lawrence roots and motivation to continue to pour pints for the community. History linked to the brewery name goes back to the 1870s and

Taps at Yankee Tank Brewing. *Courtesy of Yankee Tank Brewing, Lawrence, Kansas.*

two free staters who owned adjoining properties in Lawrence. Ezekiel Colman, an early nurseryman, nurtured berries, apples and black walnut crops on his land. He had a small stream, the Yankee Tank Creek, which emanated from his neighbor's property. Ezekiel took it upon himself to dig a pond fed by the stream to water his livestock. Back in the day, neighbors would say that the Yankee's tank was running over when heavy rain swept through the town.

The creek still runs along the K-10 highway. Check out Yankee Tank Brewery, where the beer continues to run, filling pints for the faithful fans.

7. NOT LOST BREWING COMPANY

229 South Main * Ottawa, Kansas 66067
785-214-4259
notlostbrewing.com
www.facebook.com/notlostbrewing
Brewing System: 2BBL

Once, a small fry walked into a fabric store with his mom on Main Street, no doubt thinking about what he would rather be doing. That same small fry now walks into the same building with a different mindset. Dusty Gentry, co-owner with his wife, Melody, of Not Lost Brewing Company, brews and serves his craft beer in this very building.

Melody and Dusty shared their story as time melted away. They were craft beer fans intent on using homebrewing as the platform to open a taproom brewery. Their purposeful approach combined brewing a broad range of styles, while Dusty poured over beer brewing books to enhance his skill sets. Beer fests became brewery building trips for the pair, bringing batches of their brews to share, comparing notes and learning from future professional brewers in our state ranging from Pippin and Jonathan of Sandhills Brewing to Tanner at Pathlight Brewing.

The couple have realized their dream without the help of any outside investors. They opened their doors on South Main Street in Ottawa in March 2019, giving the two close to a full year to get established before COVID-19 became the daily headline across the world. They reminisced with me about the grand opening weekend and humbly spoke about the line down the block waiting to get in, showing why their opening was the biggest in the city's history.

Oktoberfest 2021 celebration at Not Lost Brewing. *Courtesy of Not Lost Brewing, Ottawa, Kansas.*

Going it alone has made it challenging for them, as the months have slid by with the pandemic cloud still overhead. Dusty has had to go back to work, restarting his metalwork business, to keep them afloat. They are finding ways to keep the locals from leaving Ottawa for experiences elsewhere by hosting live music and trivia events. When the world gets to a better place, I hope that Not Lost Brewing Company can have its brewer, Dusty, back full time in his brewhouse.

The two are great complements to each other when it comes to what migrates on and off their beer board. Dusty has graduated from his days of knowing no beer other than Bud Light, thanks to the craft beer experiences he started sharing with Melody. His brewing style is traditional, which shows up with classics on their board ranging from the Pub Ale to the Franklin Co. Wheat. Dusty loves brewing the Surf Kansas Midwest Coast IPA, utilizing six Kansas-grown hops from bine fields within the Ottawa city limits, at Kansas Hop Company.

Melody is a supertaster, pushing the taste profiles into a range of sours and milkshake IPAs. Her ability to taste flavors with a far greater intensity balances well with Dusty's trained nose for the wonderful aromas of good beer brewing.

Expect the unexpected when you step into their taproom. Core beer styles can come and go on the eleven taps. The beauty of having a small-batch two-barrel system is the ease of brewing and introducing new styles and re-introducing core beers on their rotating tap menu. The day I visited, Dusty had finished brewing their Irish Ale, which will be tapped during the brewery's third anniversary celebration in March.

Rest assured that when you go wandering, finding your way to their front door, Melody will greet you with the melody made from her laughter. You will feel at home immediately, realizing that the wandering brought you to a taproom home away from home. I know that my wife, Ivy, and I will wander south to enjoy ourselves. I am thankful for meeting this industrious couple and appreciative of their excitement for my book, highlighted now by placement of my book sticker on a cooler door underneath their taps.

Cheers!

8. NORSEMEN BREWING COMPANY

830 North Kansas Avenue * Topeka, Kansas 66608
785-783-3999
norsemenbrewingco.com
www.facebook.com/norsemenbrewing
Brewing System: 7BBL

Visit Norsemen Brewing Company and step into a Topeka-based Valhalla. In Norse mythology, Valhalla[18] is a majestic, enormous hall located in Asgard, ruled over by the god Odin. Norsemen is a great hall ruled over by Adam and Melissa Rosdahl and Jared and Emily Rudy. The brewery is Viking in spirit with great food, an event space and some of the best beer I had across the state of Kansas. As described on the website, one can step through the doors and back in time at Norsemen Brewing Company, where all Vikings are Norsemen but not all Norsemen are Vikings.

Pint magic at Norsemen Brewing Company. *Courtesy of Norsemen Brewing Company, Topeka, Kansas.*

Enter Brad Stevens,[19] a high school classmate of mine from four decades ago and a descendant of generations of dairy farmers who worked the same land in New Hampshire. He's an owner of a 1930 Model A Ford who shares the same birthdate as me and who traveled to Kansas to join me on a segment of my book project. Norsemen Brewing was our second stop on a weekend full of good beer, friendship and long conversations as we caught up on the last four decades of life that had slid by like an Odin's One Eye IPA will easily slide down a thirsty throat.

As we walked by a group of built-out Harleys parked outside the brewery, we chuckled and looked at each other, wondering, "Are we ready for this?" Before meeting the head brewer, Brad and I had a chance to scout the tap menu, our eyes scanning across twelve styles encompassing flagship beers and a steady rotation of the latest brewhouse creations. As our pints were being poured, we caught up on facts about Odin, a war god and a god of poets who had a flowing beard and one eye (the other he gave up for wisdom). As our pints were placed in front of us, Adam Rosdahl,[20] the head brewer and reincarnation of Odin, came out to say hi. We were greeted by a guy with a long beard who had two eyes that expressed a thirst for learning and the opportunity to work his magic daily at Norsemen.

Adam's skills at brewing were sharpened through years of homebrewing with his friend and co-owner at the brewery, Jared Rudy. As their skills and equipment grew by leaps and bounds, the two were brewing more than fifteen barrels per year. Their beer was consumed at great parties where, Jared said, "We brewed and drank all day. It was so much fun."[21] The skills the two brought to the professional brewing world were developed further thanks to the graciousness and collaborative spirit that John Dean, owner and brewmaster at Topeka's Blind Tiger Brewery, extended to them. They could not learn the ropes from anyone better than John, who is a legend in the Kansas craft beer community.

My friend Brad wrote me a letter after the trip and had this to say about his time with Adam: "I really enjoyed sitting with their owner and head brewer, who was friendly and easy to talk to. Perhaps all Kansans are as well....I guess I need a few more days to know for sure."[22] One must know that Brad and his brethren in the Brentwood, New Hampshire area are known for having dry senses of humor. Later in my book journey, when I had the opportunity to sit with John Dean, he shared that he thought Adam was one of the rising brewers in the state. There is no better testimonial for those talents than to share that Dean makes a habit of stopping one night a week on his way home to have a pint and conversation with Adam.

Adam was quoted in a newspaper story when they were opening in 2016, saying that Norsemen wanted to play a part in making Topeka known for good beer. The growth of breweries in Topeka is exciting for craft beer fans in the area. Keep in mind that Adam will consistently deliver for you. He is so focused on the craft, saying to me at one point, "I like seeing where the craft came from so I can see where I am going. I am trying to learn how to play football on the field."[23]

Head brewer Adam likes to tinker, as the "Brew Like an Egyptian" story in this book captures. He is a history buff and will turn a cold trail into a hot one as he goes down rabbit holes working to perfect an ancient brew or a pre-Prohibition Kentucky common.[24] I could not help but think back to learning that Odin was a god of poetry, how the two both had long beards and the ability to craft magic with words, as Adam said, "I was doing it old western in the days of sci-fi."[25]

Skol!

9. BLIND TIGER BREWERY & RESTAURANT

417 Southwest 37th Street * Topeka, Kansas 66611
785-267-BREW (2739)
www.blindtiger.com
www.facebook.com/TheBlindTigerBreweryandRestaurant
Brewing System: 14BBL

John Dean is a storyteller. He reminisced with me about his formative years in homebrewing, which started one day when his dad caught him in the field drinking an Old Milwaukee and said, "Son, there is something better than that in the world."[26] He started trying different beer and came to the realization that ten-dollar six-packs were not working well with a six-dollar hourly wage.

Enjoy this relaxing view from a Blind Tiger Brewery barstool. *Courtesy of Blind Tiger Brewery & Restaurant, Topeka, Kansas.*

He began homebrewing in 1990, with a worn copy of Charlie Papazian's *The Complete Joy of Home Brewing*[27] under one arm, a basic homebrew kit and a recipe to brew.[28] John learned the importance of mentorship in the early days, thriving in the learning environment that the homebrewers fostered in the Greater Topeka Hall of Foamers Club.[29]

John, the most decorated brewmaster in the state, won his first white ribbon for a third-place hefeweizen. Within six years, he had started professionally brewing at Barley's Brewhouse in Topeka. He likes to say that he "did eighteen months in Leavenworth"[30] at the High Noon Saloon, winning his first medal for a raspberry wheat. John was hitting his stride, telling me, "The beauty you can find in simplicity is mind-blowing."[31] His move from the High Noon Saloon to Blind Tiger happened in 1999. In two years, the medal hit parade started.

In eighteen years, John has been recognized twenty-one times for either GABF or World Cup medals, including nine golds. His World Beer Cup medals have all come in even-ending years, which makes me feel good about his odds in 2022. I must make special note of 2014, when John and Blind

Tiger walked away with the biggest honor, winning the Champion Brewer and Champion Brewery awards, respectively, in the Large Brewpub Division.

Rest assured that when you visit Blind Tiger, you will have twenty tap options at the minimum. John loves German styling, which influences his brewing. You would think that after two decades of winning awards, John could be complacent. He is far from it. What I find amazing is that John has won medals on eleven distinctive styles! The fact that he won a medal for a basil beer highlights his continued creativity and thirst for learning. John told me, "I wake in the morning thinking, today I am going to make a beer no one on earth has ever tasted before."[32]

As John and his team (head brewer Alvaro Canizales and cellar man Connor Dean, John's son) have creatively brewed throughout the last two decades, the Blind Tiger business has continued to grow. Since 2010, the brewhouse and cellar have been expanded three times, now holding forty-one vessels. In parallel fashion, the scope of what John brews has grown to include a strong lineup of kettle sours. He had caught wind of the barrel sours early in the trend, went to every symposium possible to learn more about sours and has felt that sours have been on a trajectory for five years that could make them the new IPA.

I asked John about his openness and desire to mentor young brewers locally. He responded, "I stand on the shoulders of giants. No one gets here on their own. I had Steve Bradt at Free State and Steve Pauwels at Boulevard who helped me along the way and welcomed me into this fraternity. When I got here, I was shaking and did not want to ruin or tarnish what they were doing. I wanted to make these guys proud. I pass it along every day, nationwide and locally."[33]

One brewer John has mentored is Adam Rosdahl at Norsemen, who often stops by with a crowler of a fresh style for John to critique and enjoy. "I love his beer," he said. Norsemen is on the way home for John, so it has become a regular stop. "I drink more of his beer than mine because it is on the way home, and no one asks me to change a keg or fix a toilet!"[34]

I spent more than two hours enjoying John's company, at a table surrounded by framed photos of John with family and with legends in the brewing world at events and medal ceremonies. Within the industry, his knowledge and friendships are as legendary as his storytelling. A fitting way to bring this story home is with the hope that I have inspired you to put down my book and head to Blind Tiger.

10. HAPPY BASSET BREWING COMPANY & BARREL HOUSE

Barrel House at 510 Southwest 49th Street * Topeka, Kansas 66609
785-730-2498
Brewing Company at 29th and Wanamaker * Topeka, Kansas 66614
785-783-3688
www.happybassetbrewingco.com
www.facebook.com/HappyBassetBrewingCompany
Brewing System: 7BBL

This visit was one of firsts on an incredibly warm June 2021 day. I had a travel companion join me from New Hampshire, my high school classmate and great friend Brad Stevens, who graciously made the trip out to be part of the story. After reminiscing about our weekend together, Brad said to me, "Happy Basset Brewing was our first stop and our first beer together in way too long!" Four decades had slipped by before we reunited on this weekend. The day started at HB and ended at the K, as Brad cheered on his BoSox to a victory over our Royals.

As we sat down at the bar, we were stunned to see that the tap landscape encompassed twenty-four brews. Eric Craver, owner and brewmaster of Happy Basset Brewing, has the largest brewery tap offering in our Sunflower State. He also is one of four ownership groups in the state that is managing two thriving locations, also including Wichita Brewing Company, Defiance Brewing and Sandhills Brewing—a fifth, Transport Brewery, will join the group in the fall of 2022. A tagline for Eric's business is "Brewing Beer for Dog's Best Friend," which is so true in the case of the Craver family. The opening of their first location in 2016 was inspired by their two rescue basset hounds, named Gracie and Freckles. Since opening, the family has grown to include a third.

The next time you head to Happy Basset, take your mood temperature first. If you want a small taproom experience, go to the Wanamaker location. If you want big space, natural light, a great patio and dogs hanging out in every direction, then make your way to the 49th Street location. Brad and I had ventured to their industrial space and were immediately comfortable at what might be the longest brewery bar in the state. I cannot confirm this because I did not make a habit of traveling with a tape measure as I hit every brewery in the state!

Above: First brewery visit with high school classmate and good friend Brad Stevens at Happy Basset Brewing Company, Topeka, Kansas. *Courtesy of Happy Basset Brewing Company, Topeka, Kansas.*

Right: Introduced high school classmate Brad Stevens to the K. The Red Sox picked up a W. *Author's collection.*

Eric met us that day, sharing his story and introducing us to his original homebrew system that he artfully built, taking advantage of his metalworking talents. We learned that his twenty-plus beer styles are brewed in the two locations, with the majority brewed over at the taproom. He and the team do an excellent job of guiding patrons through three groups of beer styles, with a lineup of options available in each. As with other breweries, you can travel from easy drinking to hop country to the malty world while at Happy Basset. Make sure to follow the brewery on Facebook to see the monthly announcements regarding what new beer style will debut for the month.

Eric and his wife bring a young perspective to what they are offering, ranging from a strong lineup and rotation of music to local food trucks. The youthful vibe is so very present at their 49th Street location. The owners are expanding their brewery out there as well, transitioning into 2022 with more event space that can be used for large groups enjoying bingo, trivia night, team cornhole competitions and more. Expect good beer and a busy event calendar at Happy Basset.

I am thankful that Happy Basset was our first stop on the brewery and baseball train that day. Sampling twenty-four styles took time, which allowed me and Brad the opportunity to start reconnecting. Think about the magic that breweries like Eric's create through wonderful experiences. Beer, friends and great conversations in a comfortable and cool environment were the launching pad for a weekend of reminiscing and looking forward.

11. 785 BEER COMPANY

301 Southeast 45th Street * Topeka, Kansas 66609
Brewing System: 10BBL

For Luke and Ashley Loewen, family comes first. They have three children: Marek, Lakelyn and Lucy. As young parents know, going out is a trek because the kids are coming with you. Luke and Ashley have developed a game plan when they travel, planning out which breweries to experience wherever they may be.

Ten years ago, Ashley bought Luke his first homebrewers starter kit. The two had not started their family yet, so he had time to try to homebrew. He shared that at the time, he liked beer but "drank whatever was in the fridge in the garage."[35] The beer of choice typically was a light commercial lager like Bud Light and Natty Light. Luke has come a long way with his appreciation for beer since then.

Ashley told me that the first few batches brewed were terrible. Luke dove into the research, quickly learning that his big issue out of the gate was water quality. The effects of chloramine in the water were eliminated once he determined how to correct the quality issue. Immediately, the next batch was better. Soon, the two became obsessed with participating in the monthly Greater Topeka Hall of Foamers club homebrew meetings. This club has been the springboard for homebrewers, many of whom have gone on to have successful professional brewing careers. Think about the success that John Dean (Blind Tiger), Jared Rudy (Norsemen) and Eric Craver (Happy Basset) have had with their breweries.

Jumping ahead to 2018, we catch up with Luke and the journey. At that point, they had the most popular home on the cul-de-sac, famous for the activity on weekends, as neighbors enjoyed his good beer while they became a close community of friends.

The turning point for the two was when they started brainstorming about what they would do differently if they opened a brewery. At that moment, there was no turning back.

Luke happened to drive by the building that 785 Beer Company will call home amid their search for a location. Locals will remember the fifty-plus years that Starlite Skate Center was home to families and friends roller skating to music ranging from 1950s Motown to the beat of 1970s disco. Starlite opened back in 1966 in a location that was close to then Forbes Air Force Base. Many towns had roller rinks near military bases, catering to large populations of active military families whose favorite pastime was roller skating. I love the symmetry between the family-fun environment that has been part of the building since the mid-1960s and the family-friendly, experience-rich community gathering spot that 785 Beer Company will become.

How will 785 Beer Company be unique? Remember that this profile kicked off underscoring the importance of family to Luke and Ashley. "We want our brewery to be family focused,"[36] Ashley said to me. The brewery space will include things like three pickleball courts, a game room, event space and a full restaurant that will initially offer a limited menu, prioritizing salads and pizzas.

Luke will brew to keep eight taps busy, with plans to offer traditional lagers, ales and IPAs. One homebrew recipe that Luke plans to have on tap when they open is his cucumber cream ale, which I tried and enjoyed.

The 2021 calendar has fallen to the floor, replaced by the 2022 calendar with a floating bull's-eye, marking when 785 Beer Company might open. Think late summer or early fall, or check out the brewery online for the latest. Luke wrapped up our conversation as he talked about the name. Luke told me that for Ashley and him, their mission is to celebrate community and pride in their town and to draw visitors to Topeka.

785. Beer. Food. Friends.

12. IRON RAIL BREWING

705 South Kansas Avenue * Topeka, Kansas 66603
785-215-8123
ironrailbrewing.com
www.facebook.com/IronRailBrewing
Brewing System: 15BBL

Iron Rail Brewing celebrated its third anniversary in November 2021. It has done a wonderful job of paying homage to the rich history of Topeka and the Atchison, Topeka and Santa Fe Railroad through six striking murals spread around the brewery space. It opened in Topeka with plans to be a central part of the downtown revitalization.

In addition to the impressive murals, the brewery also has a cool visual element created by the open space looking down on the brewhouse. Stacked fermenting tanks, which has not been a common sight in my travels, appear to be peeking above the railings and beckoning visitors to grab a seat and a pint. The brewery opened with Don King as head brewer and Noah Oswald as assistant brewer. The pandemic caused Don to step away from this role, leaving Noah to take charge. Despite Noah's lack of seasoning as a brewer, his enthusiasm for the craft makes up for that. He became interested in brewing early in his childhood. In fact, he remembers watching his dad homebrew back when he was in middle school. On brew days at home, Noah would bombard his dad with questions regarding everything from the process to the type of ingredients.

Noah now manages six core beers that resulted from their early style experimentation, learning what styles appealed to their customers. The brewery just launched "Noah's Tap," which will highlight a small-batch brew with a consistent rotation of unique tastes for fans to try. One interesting story

Iron Rail Brewing mural *CKH Wheat*. Cyrus K. Holliday, founder of Topeka, is enjoying cigar and pint. Painted by Drea Nix. *Courtesy of Iron Rail Brewing, Topeka, Kansas.*

that he shared was about the "aha" moment he and Don had early in their brewing days when they realized that brewing an IPA in a top fermenting tank was challenging. Imagine climbing a ladder up to a shaky platform, standing twenty feet in the air, with a thirty-pound bag of hops to add during the dry hop process. Noah did not want to disappoint his boss in those first days and somehow overcame his fear of heights while on the platform. That same day, they decided that was their last top tank IPA!

Noah is operating solo in the brewing area, which "has been tough."[37] Once he has an assistant, Noah can reallocate time toward refining his production schedule, increasing the number of small-batch brews, finding opportunities to talk more with customers about the core beers and getting involved in specialized brewery training courses to enhance his brewing knowledge. Grab a pint and support Iron Rail and the Capital City!

13. RADIUS BREWING COMPANY

610 Merchant Street * Emporia, Kansas 66801
620-208-HOPS (4677)
radiusbrewing.com
www.facebook.com/radiusbrewing
Brewing System: 3BBL

Jeremy Johns (JJ), co-owner of Radius, a flannel-wearing and down-to-earth individual, described the ownership team as "regular dudes"[38] who, close to eight years ago, opened the doors to the third brewery to have called Emporia home. Gus Bays, co-owner and chef, while enjoying JJ's homebrew, asked if JJ would consider brewing beer in a restaurant that Gus wanted to open. The two friends were intent from day one that they would open in Emporia, a community they both loved.

Radius Brewing Company started taking shape once the two understood that they could not pull the idea off without help. Casey Woods, executive director of Emporia Main Street,[39] a nonprofit that is part of the National Main Street Program, came to them, offering assistance. JJ underscored the importance of a mantra that they have stuck with throughout their ownership of the brewery: "If we don't know how to do something, we need to find someone who does, or we can't be successful."[40]

Their brewery name originated from the idea that they wanted to keep their focus within a short radius of Emporia. JJ captured their intent perfectly, saying, "Our target market is everybody. We want to be a place that is nice enough that someone can come here for their fiftieth wedding anniversary as well as for someone getting off their tractor, feeling comfortable bellying up to the bar."[41]

Back in the late 1800s, Emporia was home to two other breweries. The first, F.H. Mackey and Son Brewery, produced more barrels of a beer in the 1870s than Radius does. The owner, born in Germany, built a cave into Perley's Hill (part of the Emporia State University campus today) and excavated one hundred feet into the hill and standing fifteen feet wide. I had to mention the volume and size of the cellar, considering that JJ has the smallest square footage three-barrel brewhouse in our state and is now approaching Mackey's volume thanks to the community's support. Mackey could not sustain a brewery that opened in a dry city, eventually shutting down as Prohibition dried out his taps.[42]

Coincidentally, within a block of Radius Brewing Company, a second brewery opened in 1879: Becker & Lincke Brewery from Leavenworth, which used this location for bottling, including its premium beer and Schlitz's Milwaukee Beer.[43]

More than a century later, the doors opened at Radius. As the team—including General Manager Chad Smith, who came on board on day one—approached their eighth anniversary in April 2022, they should feel great about their future. Unlike the defunct Mackey and Becker businesses that were short-lived back in the nineteenth century, Radius Brewing

Pints of pure magic await your arrival at Radius Brewing Company. *Courtesy of Radius Brewing Company, Emporia, Kansas.*

has drawn a crowd for its high-quality menu and beer. JJ has shifted his brewhouse responsibilities into development of new recipes while studying the latest industry and style trends, thanks to the addition of an assistant. Expect ten taps, with a large presence of flagship styles that are frequently complemented by seasonal and interesting introductions.

Community is a word with meaning for JJ. An early partnership with Emporia Main Street had significant impact on their idea becoming real. JJ told me that "being an asset to Emporia for eight years is our biggest accomplishment."[44] Today, JJ serves as the vice-president on the board for Emporia Main Street, focused on giving back, supporting new entrepreneurs and doing his part to keep Emporia vibrant and thriving.

When Radius opened in 2014, there were twenty-two breweries in our state. As I finish this book, there are more than sixty open or licensed. JJ has immersed himself in the brewing community in Kansas, doing his part to offer counsel, running a bag of grain to another brewhouse and celebrating the success of peers. As I packed up, readying myself to head to Not Lost Brewing Company in Ottawa, he made sure that I deliver a crowler of a double IPA just tapped to the owners and friends of his at Not Lost.

JJ loves how the craft beer industry has gotten more localized. Small towns and communities are embracing breweries, getting behind them with a sense of pride. That rings true at Radius Brewing Company, captured by JJ, who painted a picture of community, saying, "We have U.S. senators come in here, eating alongside the farmers that they work for."[45]

14. WILLCOTT BREWING COMPANY

219 West 4th Street * Holton, Kansas 66436
314-740-6457
www.willcottbrewing.com
www.facebook.com/willcottbrewingco
Brewing System: 20BBL

"I come from an old-school mentality,"[46] Sean Willcott, owner and brewer, opened with. "My grandpa had Willcott Liquor Store in Leavenworth, my dad had Willcott Law Office and my great-grandpa had Willcott Drug Store."[47] As I enjoy a bottle of Four Brothers IPA while writing this profile, I cannot help but think of the Willcott legacy. The authentic naming of Sean and Jennifer's brewery captures the legacy built by his ancestors, who created a reputation that was passed on generation to generation. This couple has worked incredibly hard over the last six years to bring their brewery to life.

He gutted the building to the point that four walls and four I-beams were all that remained. He and his wife, who is the "president of the whole shebang,"[48] could look up at the stars in the construction phase. As they thought about the future while stargazing, I can imagine they reflected on the life journey they started back when they met at a country stampede Aaron Tippin concert.

Jump to Christmas Day 2012 and Sean unwrapping a Mr. Beer Kit, given to him by Jared, his brother-in-law. His engineering degree from Kansas State gave him a jump on most early homebrewers. Although his first brew, a Canadian pilsner, was a disaster, Sean discovered a passion for making beer and thrived in the science behind the process. Three years later, Sean

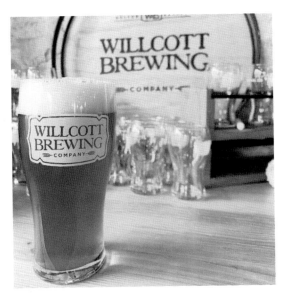

Willcott Brewing Company.
Courtesy of Willcott Brewing Company, Holton, Kansas.

and Jennifer purchased the building for the brewery after coming back to Holton from St. Louis, where he had worked as a corporate engineer for Anheuser-Busch.

Six years later, they have had four children and built a house, Jennifer has earned a master's degree while teaching in a nearby town, Sean has continued to work for a dog food manufacturing facility and, brick by brick, the brewery has reached completion. "Her sacrifices are much greater than my sacrifices,"[49] he said. This has been a true labor of love for Sean, fueling the grit and stubbornness that prevented him from walking away from the dream.

I asked Sean to tell me what they want people to remember after visiting for the first time. "I want Willcott Brewing Company to be about community, fun and relaxation,"[50] he said. Willcott Brewery prides itself on being part of a rural Kansas community and is finding ways to collaborate with other small business owners and create a space in its taproom that can host community events. The taproom will always offer its four flagship beers, complemented by a rotation of seasonal offerings. Sean brews his beer on a system that he bought from McCoy's, which at one point brewed beer at its location in Westport. His system brewed styles in the early 2000s such as Hog Pound Brown Ale, which was part of a lineup that helped open the eyes in Kansas City to the magic of craft beer.

Sean shared his thoughts on the craft beer scene, saying, "I honestly think that people don't go buy a beer because it tastes great—they buy a craft beer because of the experience. The value is not the liquid inside the bottle—the value is actually the grain itself and what does the grain stand for."[51]

As I finish my Four Brothers IPA, which is celebrating Sean and his three brothers, I know that he makes quality craft beer. Bringing great beer to his supporters is clearly something that was passed down by his grandpa. Back in the 1960s, his grandpa sued the state for not allowing chilled beer to be sold in Kansas. He won the suit and started selling chilled beer out of his liquor store, and now, more than sixty years later, Sean is serving a lineup of good craft beer to his patrons.

Family was highlighted at Willcott Brewing when my wife, Ivy, and I came to the taproom grand opening in late September 2021. The community showed up, the polka band inspired young and old to dance and his close-knit family were there, greeting supporters, pouring beer and celebrating the day with Sean, Jennifer and their children. Their fourth child was with them in spirit only. Sean and Jennifer lost their fourth child, who fought meningitis fiercely but succumbed thirty-two days after the blessing of her birth. Sean is protective of his family but was prompted by Jennifer to share the story behind their Two-Feet Wheat, which honors their inspiring angel. Losing their daughter inspired them to take on life with a passion that started their brewery journey. The understanding that they better enjoy what they do in life has been an important life lesson within their family.

Amid all the craziness of opening their brewery, the two took the time to make sure that their twelve-year-old son would receive a birthday gift that could inspire him. Jennifer shared that their son Michael had dreamed of being a cowboy and a football player for a long, long time. A twenty-four-year-old horse was soon to make a young man's life richer. After a great visit, which included a mutual agreement that I would have a book signing and talk at WB, Sean looked at me and said, "I am going home to my son to build a fence."[52]

15. MANHATTAN BREWING COMPANY

406 Poyntz Avenue * Manhattan, Kansas 66502
785-775-0406
www.mhkbeer.com
www.facebook.com/manhattanbrewing
Brewing System: 10BBL

Jake Voegeli—Kansas State graduate, center for the Wildcats football team in the early 2000s and co-owner of Manhattan Brewing Company—spelled out the core values at MBC: quality beer, beer education and community engagement. The loyal customers who have supported the MBC team since it opened in July 2020 are a strong testimonial that the values ring true. My wife, Ivy, and I immediately fell for the approach Jake described and knew that we were in for a good visit based on the warm welcome he and Adam extended to us.

How can you go wrong as a craft beer enthusiast with a beer board that has four stylistic groupings and nineteen beers on tap? Garrett Paulman and Adam Krebsbach, the brew team, pride themselves on taking their time with each brew. MBC is one of a handful of Kansas breweries that is incredibly patient with the brewing process, allowing for close to a month for each ale style to be ready. Garrett, professionally trained at Siebel Institute, brings his knowledge of process and quality control to each beer. Adam met Jake and Garrett while they all were part of the Tallgrass team. His creativity in tinkering with hops and flavor profiles shines through. Look for the beer engine at the end of the bar, as well for a chance to stretch your understanding and appreciation for the creativity that elevates good craft beer.

As I mentioned earlier, this team built their skill sets at Tallgrass, which closed its doors in 2018. Garrett told the other two that there was no better time to open a brewery than when they were unemployed. Finding the building took time, as did naming the brewery. They uncovered interesting history behind the name, first used in Chicago when Al Capone owned

Check out the great beer selection at Manhattan Brewing Company. *Author's collection.*

Manhattan Brewing.[53] The name was brought back to life in New York City in the 1980s in one of the first brewpubs on the East Coast, home to head brewer Garrett Oliver. Oliver went on to make a name for himself when he opened Brooklyn Brewing and became the only brewer in the world to have won the James Beard Award. Jake talked about their logo and script design and how they paid homage to the history of Manhattan Brewing Company.

The love for Manhattan is evident within the brewery. Step into a building that has the Wildcat color aesthetics as well as great sight lines to the brewhouse. Step up to the bar, made of purpleheart wood, an incredible hardwood with South American origins that, when cut, turns into a deep eggplant color. Look around and you will notice a Wildcat football helmet on display, autographed by Jordy Nelson. Jake is intent to get more former players engaged with MBC.

Manhattan Brewing Company stands among a small group of breweries across the Kansas craft beer community with its monthly commitment to supporting different nonprofit causes and local needs. Have a pint of its special pour and know that your dollar is one of many collected for causes such as the Brew for the Zoo, Valor Honey and the Special Olympics. Jake spoke with awe about how packed the brewery is whenever they have a cause-driven event.

This was the first brew tour visit with my wife, Ivy, as my travel companion. The team at this outstanding brewery smiled as Ivy congratulated them for serving her the best beer she had ever had. Adam had artfully walked us through all nineteen tasters, describing the hops, aromas and flavor profiles. As we sat on the patio, planning when we would come back to MBC, she jokingly said to me, "How many Fridays can I take off?"[54]

Ivy walked away with a deep appreciation for what breweries such as Manhattan Brewing do for their communities and the craft and artistry that brew teams use to deliver great beer.

16. 15-24 BREW HOUSE

420 Lincoln Avenue * Clay Center, Kansas 67432
785-777-1524
www.1524brewhouse.com
www.facebook.com/1524brewhouse
Brewing System: 10BBL

View from the 15-24 Brew House bar, in Clay Center, Kansas. *Author's collection.*

"Isn't that silly?!"[55] Clint Armstrong, owner and brew master, exclaimed as he watched my wife, Ivy, and I react to our first taste of Ope Milkshake IPA. Clint went on to say that the experience should take one back to being a kid and eating an orange Creamsicle. Our time at 15-24 Brew House in downtown Clay Center was rich in the storytelling, full of flavorful beer notes and so chill as Clint and the team took care of us.

Clay Center is full of surprises for first-time visitors. It is a rural Kansas town in flux, winning the battle to stay viable and interesting more than it is losing. We walked into Brew House, raving about the "Mural Movement" that is thriving within the town center. A band of talented artists has painted close to twenty murals on surfaces ranging from sides of buildings to grain silos that draw day-trippers to stop in this off-the-beaten-path town with close to four thousand residents.

Make a point of including 15-24 as you stop for a good beer and meal on your next day trip. You will walk into a casual brewhouse that has one of the best playlists in any Kansas brewery thanks to Clint's passion complemented by his manager, Phil Kasper, who is a local DJ and music genius. The link to music is in the production facility as well. Clint, who always has a story ready to share, described why certain album covers were located on specific vessels. The first vessel he owned is graced with the Eagles' *Hotel California* album cover. His top beer, the One-Eye Open IPA, is in the Allman Brothers' *Eat a Peach* tank. Combining his favorite beer with his favorite all-time album captures the magic and passion that Clint brings to his customers, with a packed tap list of twelve to fourteen styles. Clint talked about his professional brewing journey, saying, "I have tried so many things that I know what is going to work. I use my own scientific backbone and experience in creating something that is approachable, drinkable and good, something that I am proud of."[56]

I am always looking to learn more about brewing families. Clint was quick to call his wife, Sarah, "the brains in the family."[57] She is the mom of three daughters and principal at a local school, closing in on her doctorate in 2022. The couple embraces a key phrase in the Allman Brothers song "Eat a Peach": "I ain't a-wastin' time no more, 'cause time goes by like pouring rain."[58]

What is next for Clint and 15-24? The good news is that he has received tremendous support from his patrons. When my wife and I sat with him in July, he talked about how every month in 2021, the brewhouse set a record for the highest sales month since it opened in late fall of 2018. Good business grounded on great beer and a strong menu is making the next round of dreams worth considering. There might be a day in 2022 when we enjoy sitting outside at its beer garden patio, listening to live music or playing a competitive game of cornhole. On top of that, Clint is brewing three times a week just to keep up with his demand. Scaling up production in new space is another possibility.

Clint's brewing story started with a homebrew version of the "Tire," developed further through Siebel Institute classes; his first brewery experience is now embellished by a handful of beer festival medals. "I love small breweries,"[59] Clint said. Opening in Clay Center was meant to be for the Armstrong family. "Our philosophy is to bring the town up,"[60] he mentioned as he leaned on the *Hotel California* tank. In the background as we spoke, I could faintly hear a unique spin on the song itself.

Plenty of room at the 15-24
Any time of week
You can find the brew here

17. RIVERBANK BREWING

13 West Main Street * Council Grove, Kansas 66846
www.riverbankbrewing.com
www.facebook.com/riverbankbrewing
Brewing System: 3BBL

"Super cool" captures the essence of what is happening at 13 West Main Street in Council Grove, a town of just under 2,100 people. Riverbank Brewing officially opened its doors on November 12, 2021. We need to

Pint inviting you to sit at the Riverbank Brewing bar. *Courtesy of Riverbank Brewing, Council Grove, Kansas.*

celebrate the incredible efforts of the five owners in their "spare time" who created this community space. Deidre and Jesse Knight, Lindsay and Joshua Gant and Pat Atchity are juggling the magic building at Riverbank, with their full-time jobs ranging from social media/marketing to supply chain management to teaching and coaching at a high school level. After meeting Deidre for the first time, she looked around the space and chuckled as she told me, "It didn't look anything like it does now."[61] This team, which came together because of a common interest in making a difference in Council Grove, put a ton of sweat equity into their space, tackling all aspects of the interior work.

Jesse and Deidre bought this building back in 2017. The building that had started as a livery stable evolved through the next hundred years as a skating rink, bowling alley and armory. The structure sat empty for close to thirty years before they stepped in. Jesse and Deidre took a chance on this space, having the vision of establishing a small screen print business next door to help cover some costs associated with the brewery buildout. Picture the rainy afternoon that the two went to their building and discovered the rain coming down as hard inside as it was outside. Deidre and Jesse said to each other, "We are in a lot of trouble."[62]

The team worked for two years writing grant proposals, looking for financing to close the gap between what their bank was comfortable loaning them and their needs, which had increased because of major structural projects. The key catalyst that pushed the project across the finish line was the Founders Club, created by the team with the hope that financial support from the community would close the gap. Breweries create communities, exemplified by the more than one hundred community members, local businesses, family and friends across the country who became Riverbank Brewing club members. This amazing story of a community joining hands to raise the roof is an example of why Council Grove was recognized in 2021 by *Smithsonian Magazine* as one of the fifteen best small towns in America.[63]

The Riverbank team "wants people to know what it feels like to live here, to visit here." Step up to the bar and check out the sixteen taps available. Offerings will range from Riverbank craft beer to guest beer to craft cocktails. Snacks ranging from charcuterie boards to locally made pretzels will add to the enjoyment had by all. Rest assured that Deidre and Joshua, who share brewing responsibilities, will bring you familiar beer stylings that will stand out above other breweries because they strive to use Kansas grains, hops and local seasonal ingredients to deliver a pint that will be memorable.

Riverbank comes alive when these doors open. The energy and joy that can be felt within the brewery space and outside on the riverbank patio are contagious.

18. KANSAS TERRITORY BREWING COMPANY

310 C Street * Washington, Kansas 66968
785-510-6038
www.kansasterritorybrewingco.com
www.facebook.com/Kansas-Territory-Brewing-Company
Brewing System: 320BBL

"I want to be the Yuengling of the Midwest,"[64] said Brad Portenier, owner of Kansas Territory Brewing Company, when asked what his vision was for his new brewery location south of downtown Washington. For me, it was a day of extremes, starting with this visit and ending with hours of travel across the state during a day of dangerously high winds, dust storms and tragic plains fires.

I was quick to appreciate that I was stepping foot into the largest production facility in the state of Kansas and perhaps the largest single-owned craft brewery in the country. Talk about scale. Brandon Gunn, head brewer, graciously walked me through the facility, describing how he learned the intricacies of the high-tech system that is now his baby. Brandon grew up as a brewer during his time at Tallgrass when it had significant growth. He knows scale but was quick to admit that at times he was still intimidated as his team started scaling up production in this brewhouse.

Kansas Territory Brewing Company. "Listen to your LIFE COACH and suck it up." *Courtesy of Kansas Territory Brewing Company, Washington, Kansas.*

Brad, who is a friend to everyone, handed me the second can of beer to come off the eighteen-head, auto-pack canning line at the new location. He and I first met when I stopped in unannounced one night for a pint at the original taproom and had a Brad encounter when he walked up to me and warmly challenged me, saying, "I don't know you."[65] I gave him the same response, and so goes the beginning of our relationship. I grew to appreciate Brad's drive to do more and to think on an even grander scale as he explained the setup of the brewery and the view from the patio that will overlook his new 2,500-gallon distillery. Expect live music in the amphitheater and views of distillery barrels rolling down train tracks.

Brandon's focus will be different than most head brewers across the state. His production facility is high tech, and his lineup of craft beers is set (led by the Life Coach brew), thus he takes on a leadership role focused on the operations and day-to-day overall management of Kansas Territory. The scale of this brewery distances him from the intimacy of brewing that most head brewers experience in their smaller production facilities across Kansas.

Brad and his wife, Donna, own Bradford Built, a company that has grown tremendously over the last twenty-seven years. The production facility is a stone's throw from the new brewery location. When I asked him why they landed in Washington, a rural Kansas community of just under 1,100 people, he was quick to quip, "People are like barn swallows,"[66] which keep coming back. Indeed, Brad came back to his hometown, which has been a consistent theme in my brewery visits across the state. We wrapped up the visit with a discussion about community and the significant role that Kansas Territory can have in Washington and the region. Brad did not disappoint, capturing how grand moments can be in breweries such as his, saying that "a warm Falstaff in the right company is indeed an incredible beer!"[67]

Brewery cooler doors are sticker mosaics. *Author's collection.*

Chapter 5

BREWERY 101

had the opportunity to hang out with Sam McClain, brewmaster at Lawrence Beer Company on the east side of Lawrence, in late 2021. My goal was to write a feature focused on how each of us can enjoy our brewery visits with a greater understanding of what is happening in the brewhouse. Sam's mantra as you enter any brewery across our great state is, "Do not be intimidated."[1]

As you walk into a brewery, walk in with the awareness that you are in a place where you can spend time together, drink a beer you like, make new friends and have a wonderful experience. Sam summed up the same feeling when he shared a key ethos of LBC. "Our brewery's philosophy is different from others; whatever you are into you can find."[2] Sam went on to say that LBC's ideal customer experience is when "someone in our neighborhood wants a beer, walks down the block, has a pint, meets a friend and goes home."[3]

Next time you go to a brewery, have fun checking out the production side of the brewery. Thanks to the window views, a design element found across most breweries, today you can find a view of the brewhouse equipment and setup. Pause as you glance at the production space.

Each brewery will have a brewing and cellar area. Look for the brewing area, known as the brewhouse or hot side. You will see a tight collection of tanks with controls that manage the start of the brewing process. This is where the brewer introduces the malted barley or wheat, water, hops and yeast to one another. The milling of the grain has occurred, setting

Lawrence Beer Company logo.
Courtesy of Lawrence Beer Company.

the brewer up to orchestrate the mash of the four ingredients and the boil of the wort. Remember Sam's advice not to be intimidated by the environment? The wort is the beer before it moves to the cellar; you can think of it as a hoppy, malted tea! Amazingly, the brewing process typically takes just six hours.

The cool aspect of the brewing world is that all breweries do the same things and in the same way, whether brewing Natural Light or a high-ABV imperial stout. Each brewery's unique styles are an output from its recipes, the different ingredients, timing of introduction and brewing process. "Look for the cellar with the tanks with conical bottoms,"[4] guided Sam in our conversation. Based on the scale of each brewery and its production space, you will see different cellar sizes. The larger cellars, with more conditioning tanks with the conical bottoms, are advantageous to a brewer interested in delivering a wide range of styles to you, from classic IPAs to flagship lagers.

The smaller-sized breweries are limited in style range. Why? The fermenting or conditioning tanks are active, with yeast strains transforming the beer to hit the aromas, flavors and body in a recipe. Cellaring can take as few as ten days and as long as sixteen weeks, depending on the style of beer, until the beer is tapped. Lagers sit in the cellar due to their lower temperatures and longer fermentation cycle. A brewmaster who has a limited number of vessels in its cellar must be careful with the production schedule. If he ties up one of his few tanks with a lager, it will affect his ability to keep style selection at its optimum for his customers. Tying up one of the two or three tanks prevents the brewery from replenishing flagship styles or new introductions.

At LBC, "most of the flagship beers are brewed four to five times a year."[5] I must confess that at this point in authoring this story, I headed straight to the fridge to grab a pint of his session IPA, fondly called "East Side" by LBC's fans. Sam went on to tell me that "even in a span of a year, we only have four to five chances to tweak recipes."[6] The adjustments that Sam makes through the year are driven by availability of ingredients. An important principle for the team is that "the standard is to be true to brand with their flagship beers."[7] The changes made need to be in the background of the taste and aroma, so each pint consumed hits the mark for that given style.

The LBC team is not beholden to distributor demands for more kegs and six-packs because it decided not to go that route. This is where Sam gets excited. Each week, his goal is to determine what beers to brew to keep his flagship styles coming to his customers, while also having the freedom to "freestyle" at times like Patrick Mahomes does for the Kansas City Chiefs. "We can brew what we want when we want to,"[8] Sam declared.

Shift your attention to Servaes Brewing Company in Shawnee, where Courtney Servaes is one of the state's best freestylers. Her focus is to deliver what her community is asking for, which has led her brewery to brew sours galore. Her customers flock to this taproom environment, which is a different model than what Sam is part of at LBC. The entire focus at Servaes is to provide a community gathering spot that is approachable, while also challenging her fans with something new constantly as she rotates her taps.

Courtney has a much smaller brewhouse than LBC, but as Sam described, the brewing process remains the same. No matter what brewery you visit, the uniqueness of its style approach is driven by what we, the customers, drink. Where Courtney separates Servaes Brewing from LBC is through her recipes, her ingredients used and her approach to the number of taps by style. Sours could represent close to 40 percent of her taps, while Sam and LBC concentrate on a larger share of IPAs for their community.

Courtney and Servaes Brewing Company are one of thirteen breweries along the Ale Trail, which follows in the next chapter. Have fun visiting these breweries, which will offer you opportunities to discover new styles, techniques and gathering spots to hang out. The Ale Trail breweries are in Johnson County, the fastest-growing county in our state. Expect at least two new breweries to open on the trail in 2022, including Friction Beer Company in Shawnee and Stockyards Brewing Company in Overland Park. As you discover new tastes and develop a style preference, there is no doubt you will have a favorite neighborhood brewery along the trail ready to pour a pint to your liking.

Servaes Brewing Company's front door logo to its Shawnee, Kansas taproom. *Author's collection.*

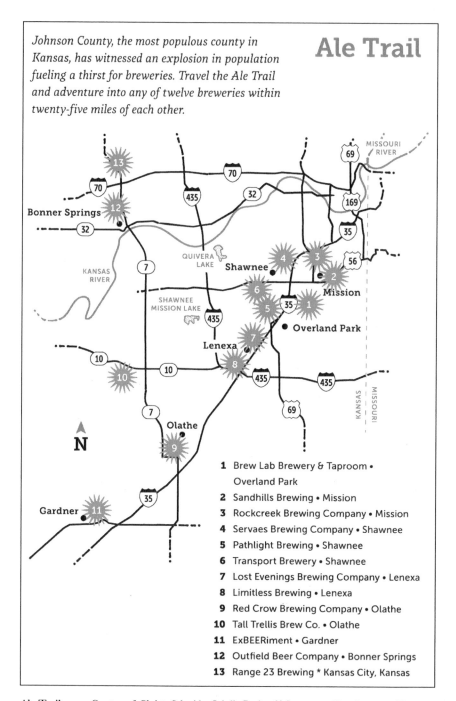

Johnson County, the most populous county in Kansas, has witnessed an explosion in population fueling a thirst for breweries. Travel the Ale Trail and adventure into any of twelve breweries within twenty-five miles of each other.

Ale Trail

1 Brew Lab Brewery & Taproom • Overland Park

2 Sandhills Brewing • Mission

3 Rockcreek Brewing Company • Mission

4 Servaes Brewing Company • Shawnee

5 Pathlight Brewing • Shawnee

6 Transport Brewery • Shawnee

7 Lost Evenings Brewing Company • Lenexa

8 Limitless Brewing • Lenexa

9 Red Crow Brewing Company • Olathe

10 Tall Trellis Brew Co. • Olathe

11 ExBEERiment • Gardner

12 Outfield Beer Company • Bonner Springs

13 Range 23 Brewing * Kansas City, Kansas

Ale Trail map. *Courtesy of Christy Schneider, Inkello Design & Letterpress, East Lawrence, Kansas.*

Chapter 6

THE ALE TRAIL

1. BREW LAB BREWERY + KITCHEN

7925 Marty * Overland Park, Kansas 66204
913-400-2343
www.brewlabkc.com
www.facebook.com/brewlabkc
Brewing System: 3BBL

Visit Brew Lab in Overland Park and witness the definition of lab ring true. The ownership team has watched the homebrewing scene in Johnson County lose its luster; class enrollment for its homebrewing classes also has shrunk. As the Ale Trail in JoCo has exploded,[1] the ability for any craft beer fan to visit a neighborhood brewery nearby has blossomed. Josh Turpin, one of the co-owners of Brew Lab, mentioned that they continue to focus on experimenting and changing the space based on trends and insights that will continue to set Brew Lab apart from its Ale Trail neighbors.

The leadership team, comprising four friends with diverse professional backgrounds, has not hesitated to evolve Brew Lab and what it offers, catering especially to the neighborhood. One of the key assets that the brewery has is space. Brew Lab has a record of successful events, ranging from crowded and boisterous trivia nights to live music, corporate events and hosting nationally known comedy acts.

Brew Lab Brewery + Kitchen, located in Overland Park, Kansas. *Author's collection.*

The brewery space will evolve in 2022, with expansion of the brewhouse capabilities a top priority, followed by introducing more taproom seating and a permanent patio space. Expansion of brewhouse capabilities is essential as the team gets ready to introduce a late summer Brew Lab beer release. The fresh style will be supported by special tap handles and marketing efforts, which will be available in the taproom, as well as in local bars and restaurants. Kevin Combs, co-owner, excitedly shared, "We are going to fill a much-needed hole in local tap handles."[2]

The changes would not be possible if not for the full kitchen and robust menu offering, complemented by eighteen taps showcasing Brew Lab styles, thanks to the efforts of Charley Olson, head brewer. Kevin, assistant brewer extraordinaire, shared, "We've shifted our focus over the years from being an experimental brewery with a few flagships to perfecting our best beers, while continuing to introduce fun, experimental styles."[3] Charley will continue to push monthly introductions in addition to seasonal styling to keep their fans happy with opportunities to try new things.

The fact that each co-owner has specific professional strengths and Brew Lab responsibilities alleviates pressure on any one of them, considering that they maintain full-time roles as an ecommerce business entrepreneur (Josh), industrial real estate developer for Insight Commercial (Kevin), college professor at Benedictine College (Clay Johnston) and an accountant (Justin Waters) who also is in the Coast Guard Reserves.

Brew Lab Brewery has a legacy to celebrate that has given craft beer fans a chance to enjoy breweries up and down the Ale Trail. Kevin said, "Brew Lab has touched almost all of the local Johnson County breweries in one way or another. We were paramount in the evolution of Johnson County's craft beer scene. We were there in the beginning and watched our homebrewers became pros of their own."[4]

Communities are created in breweries such as Brew Lab, as well as in the Ale Trail brewery family; Kevin emphasized, "We have a common mission which is to produce great craft beer for our local community to enjoy."[5]

2. SANDHILLS BREWING

5612 Johnson Drive * Mission, Kansas 66202
913-204-0080
sandhillsbrewing.com
www.facebook.com/sandhillsbrewingmission
Brewing System: 3½BBL

This is a delightful story about twin brothers—as well as best friends—who grew up in a close-knit family amid the Sand Hills. Each child in the family was given a name linked to nature, with Pippin and Jonathan honoring varieties of apples. Their deep appreciation of the natural environment no doubt grew as they spent lazy summer afternoons exploring the dunes, trails and grassland prairie for which the Sand Hills are famous. That love is on exhibit today, shining through at their breweries.

Why are there two locations? It comes back to the love the two brothers have for each other and where they live. They have had symmetrical professional journeys, both owning and leading online gaming companies. They even opened the location in Mission one year later to the day than in Hutchinson. The brewery business has kept Pippin in Hutch and Jonathan in KC while minimizing the miles separating the two, as they are in constant daily contact while managing the business.

Two brothers, two locations and, in ways, two unique audiences. The Chickadee Berliner Weisse is the top beer in Hutch, while the Junco New England IPA is the pint of choice in the Mission location. Both styles celebrate different bird species, as do all core beers in the Sandhills lineup. Count on Sandhills to stretch your taste buds with an array of barrel-aged

Snowy day, great pint, and patio weather. *Courtesy of Sandhills Brewing in Mission, Kansas.*

beers. Top of the list for the team today is a passion for oak-aged beer that they discovered as they watched brewers experiment with oak-aged pilsners. Rest assured that the brothers strive to have an option available for whatever your palate leans toward, including a barrel-aged style on any day you visit.

What I found striking about the approach Pippin and Jonathan share has been their purpose-driven focus on building a brewery business that will last for decades to come. Sandhills Brewing will age well because of the discipline they have brought over from their other businesses. Consistency for customers when any of the eight taps are pulled is essential. Pippin went on to share, "More than anything, if you want to be somewhere long-term, you have to start planning for that early on. It's the overall mindset, thinking long-term so you can make better, more thoughtful decisions that is important."

When you visit Sandhills on a Friday or Saturday, take advantage of the Johnson Drive patio, a pint and the sun blessing you with warmth and energy. The Mission location is a comfortable taproom with a great view of the brewhouse. Check out the tap board to see what birds are perched and waiting for you. Jonathan has created the same neighborhood feel along the Ale Trail that is the drawing card for beer fans looking for the opportunity for conversation, company and a cold one.

3. ROCKCREEK BREWING COMPANY

5880 Beverly Avenue * Mission, Kansas 66202
913-218-0017
rockcreekbrewingco.square.site
www.facebook.com/rockcreekbrewingco
Brewing System: 10BBL

The Fab Five, who shared the hallways for years at the North KC Cerner headquarters, decided that their dream of owning a craft brewery could indeed come true. The band of brewers—Mark Schonhoff and his wife, Sara Charlson; Craig Reed; Chris Murrish; and Sameer Brahmavar—became enthusiastic about homebrewing, enriching their knowledge and skills while visiting craft breweries during their travels.

Finding the right location took three years but resulted in a cool space just off the main drag in Mission, on the edge of a quiet neighborhood. Despite the shutdown during the pandemic, Rockcreek has established a tightknit community since their May 2020 opening, one that thoroughly enjoys hanging out in great indoor and outside patio spaces.

The late Friday afternoon that I visited with my in-law, Kevin, the brewer was tasting a pint at the bar while the Fab Five and friends were getting together over a pint amid the brewery community. The team highlights an important motto that they lived by during their decades at Cerner, which they have brought with them to this new chapter in their lives:

#Work hard. Play hard. DrinKC.

Pouring a pint at Rockcreek Brewing Company. *Courtesy of Rockcreek Brewing Company, Mission, Kansas.*

The craft brewery was recognized by *Pitch KC* in 2020 as the "Best New Brewery" because of its great space, vibrant community and good beer. Speaking of beer, the brewer, Trent Wiegers, has a brewhouse capable of keeping ten beers on tap. Rockcreek's fans clearly are enjoying his beer, considering that Trent brewed his 100th batch in December 2021. The team's approach is to maintain a good mix of fan favorite core beers, interspersed with seasonal and unique styles. You will not be left without a choice when visiting Rockcreek, as Trent has thoughtfully approached variety across key beer styles.

We should support Rockcreek because of how focused the team is on being an integral part of Mission and the local community. The ownership team made the strategic decision to pay their staff a reasonable salary without tips from day one. Know that the tips you leave behind for Rockcreek are collected on a quarterly basis to support local charitable groups or foundations. I was proud to leave a tip in support of its Q1 fundraiser supporting the family of Chuck Marksbury, who was admitted to a hospital in December 2021 due to COVID complications.

Stop in after working hard at your job for a pint of your favorite beer. Step through the doors next to play hard and enjoy friends and family at Rockcreek Brewing Company. The leadership team honors the local craft beer scene with the last words in their motto, "DrinKC." Have a pint or two, laugh until your voice is lost and know that as you leave a tip behind, you are helping improve the quality of life of those in need in Mission and the local community.

4. SERVAES BREWING COMPANY

10921 Johnson Drive * Shawnee, Kansas 66203
913-608-5220
www.servaesbrewco.com
www.facebook.com/servaesbrewingco
Brewing System: 7BBL

"I was interested in the movement, the experience and the friendship,"[6] Courtney Servaes said as she described the first Lawrence Brewers Guild meeting she attended. "That was the beginning of everything."[7] Courtney thanks Angelo Ruiz—a member of the guild, head brewer for Yankee Tank and a good friend—for bringing her into the brewery world. Typical of this amazing brewing community, she and Angelo explored tastes by trying craft brewery selections while starting to brew together. After co-brewing a dozen times, Courtney made her first homebrew, a pumpkin beer that she thought was amazing at the time—she laughs now as she looks back with an evolved perspective.

Courtney started shaping her brewing style, which was noticed early by other homebrewers, winning awards recognizing her emerging, innovative talents. She had a thirst for learning and a wife, Brandi, who encouraged her to venture into the uncharted kettle sour styles. Typically, a patron will have seven to eight sour options on the board, balanced with a group of traditional style offerings. No brewery in our state has a daily sour assortment like Servaes Brewing. Her creativity is mind-blowing, as she adds whole pumpkin pies, chocolate chip cookies and other interesting ingredients to her brews. Courtney has forged a unique position in the state with her approach, offering depth in a style category that most do not.

"I never wanted flagships. I didn't want to brew the same beer over and over again,"[8] Courtney shared. She maps out her brewing schedule, building in the fluidity to try new things and constantly reinvent the beer. Her loyal customers frequent the taproom more than might be common in other breweries, intrigued by what is on the tap rotation, knowing that they will be surprised.

Family was a central theme in our conversation. Courtney met her wife while they both were working at Ottawa University. They have two sons, Aaron and Dylan, who keep them busy. In fact, the focus on creating an environment for everyone at the taproom is exemplified through the line of brewed soda options under the label Aaron's Craft Sodas. His experience

Enjoy Servaes Brewing Company's taproom and selection of flavor-forward beer, located in Shawnee. *Author's collection.*

when traveling to breweries became fuller the first time he was able to order a brewery root beer. He worked with Courtney to create soda flavors in advance of Servaes opening its doors in 2019.

"Brewed by a girl" is a rotating banner on the Servaes web page. Courtney is the first female brewer and owner among the Kansas craft brewery community today. As 2021 ended, three more female brewers joined the ranks, including Kaydee and Laura at Ladybird and Deidre at Riverbank. I asked John Dean, owner and brewmaster at Blind Tiger, what he remembers about women in Kansas brewing since his start in the 1990s. He recalled several female assistant brewers back in the mid-1990s at breweries such as Barley's Brewery, Little Apple Brewing Company and High Noon Saloon & Brewery.

I am hopeful that as the craft brewery scene in Kansas continues to grow, we will see an infusion of more women brewers, as well as growth in the number of women who own or share ownership of Sunflower State breweries.[9] The Kansas brewery industry is behind the curve versus the overall U.S. industry, including adopting beer style trends more quickly and accelerating the share and number of women in our state's brewing industry. Entering the Kansas brewing community was not a big hurdle for Courtney, which has been a similar experience for her peers. Nationally, there have been awful stories about women encountering sexist hurdles and experiences that must be eliminated.

Courtney is a pioneer in our state, making space for herself as a good brewer among the many in Kansas, setting an example for those women who might be considering chasing a dream in the world of brewing. Celebrate Courtney, her brewery and her focus on a medley of flavors when you visit Shawnee!

5. PATHLIGHT BREWING

11200 West 75th Street * Shawnee, Kansas 66214
913-400-2615
www.pathlightbrewing.com
www.facebook.com/PathlightBrewing
Brewing System: 50BBL

David Harris and Tanner Vaughn became style experts in their homebrewing days, one in pursuit of the next great IPA while the other tinkered and obsessed over barrel-aged beers and wild ales. Their shared passion slowly overwhelmed David's wife, Beth, who finally succumbed to the thought of opening a brewery after two years of conversations. Thus, the path was lit and the journey began.

The success at Pathlight has been forged by a trio focused on the community of Shawnee, the community at Pathlight and the welcoming environment that caters to families, Formula One racing fans and patio dogs. I had company the day I visited: joining me were my daughter Meaghan and my six-month-old granddaughter, Luna. We were incredibly fortunate to have one of the best tasting experiences during this book project. Tanner sat with us as we took the Pathlight journey, tasting every beer as we did, sharing thoughts on the methodologies, the recipes, the pursuit of balanced beer, the dialing-in of the recipes and his brewing education. His passion and talent lit up our experience, which included a granddaughter determined to try her first IPA!

I encourage you to get to know David, Beth and Tanner on your first of what will be repeat visits. Their openness, commitment to excellence and thirst for conversation and community building will result in a newfound

Pathlight Brewing Company, home to beer crafted by Tanner Vaughn. *Courtesy of Pathlight Brewing Company, Shawnee, Kansas.*

loyalty to Pathlight. Tanner is easy to spot. Look for the guy known as the "Mad Brewer" who is in the Carhartt overalls, working hard, giving great care to the largest barrel aging program in the state. If you can have a conversation with Tanner, you will walk away richer for the experience and inspired by his passion.

David is the IPA hophead, a dad of two daughters who is heavily engaged in helping to make the KC community stronger. Tanner is the Yoda, a man with multiple degrees, a thirst to learn and a humbleness when witnessing how the Pathlight community digs his great beer. As Tanner walked us through the operation, he spoke about the ten-gallon system that he had in his basement and the three hundred gallons he would brew per year. He is exceptional at what he does because of his professional background. He has a facility for chemistry, ranging from crystalline structures to the form of explosives in a weapon system he worked on while at Honeywell.

Tanner's brew days started back in college when he found a way around the campus rules about buying beer by discovering that there were no stipulations about *brewing* beer. Yes, he did get in trouble for his efforts, but they paid off from the first brew: a vanilla porter. Tanner is enthusiastic about lagers, English and German traditional ales, saisons and barrel-aged brewing and the intricacies in yeast management. He spoke about his enjoyment of drier beers and the influence his Philadelphia travel and introduction to Yuengling had on him.

One can expect to deliberate over thirteen tap choices on a Pathlight visit. The influence of the ownership is evident. David's love of IPAs and the journey of finding a balance between great aroma and a touch of bitterness show up on the tap list. Beth influences Tanner's brew schedule to make sure there is always at least one style that has a higher ABV coupled with rich flavors. Tanner is committed to rotating the styles offered as fast as possible; rest assured that he wants to have something available for everyone. His hopes for the future in the Kansas craft beer scene are that people accept lagers as good craft beer again, as well as seeing traditional English and German styles become popular in our state.

Tanner is the second brewer I have met with synesthesia,[10] which influences their brewing. The innate skill he discussed with me blew my mind. Picture this: beer flavors playing music, which Tanner then turns into pictures and colors. "I am always working to write a better song. I often memorize beers by pictures. I can memorize my recipes and flavor palate of the beer and take colors out and apply them to a different painting to change the next recipe."[11]

Tanner grounds what he does every day in techniques that go back to the Germans and the English, while constantly learning and experimenting in pursuit of making great craft beer. Combine that with the intimate details he shared about his artistry in pursuing another hit song and one can rest assured that he will introduce something beautiful.

We closed our visit by listening to Tanner talk about the importance of having a philosophy for why one owns a brewery or is a brewer. For the team at Pathlight, the focus on community engagement and immersion, the goal of creating a comfortable place for people to be in the moment and the desire to collaborate with other breweries across the state to strengthen the craft beer scene are the tenets of their shared philosophy. Our breweries and brewers across the state share a simple philosophy that if they all continue to make a better product, we collectively will reap the benefits!

My daughter Meaghan looked at me as we packed up Luna and said, "I want to do this again tomorrow!"[12]

6. TRANSPORT BREWERY

11113 Johnson Drive * Shawnee, Kansas 66203
913-766-6673
www.transportbrewery.com
www.facebook.com/transportbrewery
Brewing System: 6BBL

Get ready to truly connect with your beer when you visit Transport Brewery. The team of bartenders, led by General Manager Christie Merandino, is unique within the Kansas craft beer scene. Each team

Lose your hat after a few great pints at Transport Brewery, Shawnee, Kansas. *Courtesy of Johnson County Brewing Company LLC.*

member goes through a Cicerone Certification program within their first six months at the brewery, which positions them with a beer knowledge that can make your experience that much richer. The brewery, owned by a group led by Mike McVey and Jason Leib, was the first to open in Shawnee. The team, inspired by Kansas City and the transportation hub that emanates from Kansas City, decided to celebrate that through the naming of the brewery. Count on Transport to have close to half a dozen core beers on tap, with another six taps dedicated to seasonal offerings. The team was fortunate to have Sean Greenwood come on board in the last year as another partner and brewer. Trained as a chemist, Sean is bringing traditional English beer styles to the Transport followers, including a cask beer rotation and a taproom beer engine.

Amazingly, Transport opened in a community within Johnson County that seventy years ago had a population of 5,000. Today, JoCo is the second-largest county in the state, with a population of more than 610,000![13] Transport Brewery opened with no brewery neighbors. Close to three years later, you can enjoy a section of the JoCo Ale Trail, with Servaes Brewing and Pathlight Brewing located within two and a half miles of each other. Friction Brewing will be coming to the neighborhood in 2022 as the Ale Trail continues to explode.

The evolution of breweries in this county makes me think of the core group of breweries in the Wichita Way area. After opening in downtown Shawnee, the Transport team has Pathlight, Rock Creek, Sandhills, Lost Evenings and Limitless Brewing nearby. As the community of breweries has grown, their support and collaboration mirror the spirit I have seen within the core group of Wichita breweries. The fact that these breweries focus on growing the industry within our state bodes well for us as fans. Great beer and incredible community gathering spots grounded with a midwestern vibe cannot be beat.

The followers of Transport have grown since they opened. The owners found this historic footprint and have created an eclectic, comfortable pub vibe to enjoy. The magic is reminiscent of a Cheers environment. Jason finds the experience of hanging out in the taproom surreal. He and Mike started brainstorming about opening a brewery close to seven years ago. By the end of 2022, the Transport ownership team will be opening their second location in Gardner.

The challenge for the team as it continues to grow will be to capture the magic of the local pub feel in Shawnee at the second location as well. One cannot beat entering a taproom such as Transport with your favorite bartender saying, "Can I pour you a pint of the Post-It Note Pale Ale?"

7. LOST EVENINGS BREWING COMPANY

8625 Hauser Street * Lenexa, Kansas 66215
913-766-0333
www.losteveningsbrewingcompany.com
www.facebook.com/LostEveningsBrewing
Brewing System: 3½BBL

Pat and Heather Davis wanted their brewery name to connect with their love of music. Pat mentioned that one of his favorite artists is Frank Turner, a British folk/punk singer. "I was looking for a name and it hit me that the lyrics from a Turner song were perfect."[14] Their brewery name jumped out from the powerful lyrics: "Life is about love, last minutes and lost evenings."[15]

Pat and Heather are another one of these dynamic couples who have full-time professional careers they are balancing with realizing their dream of opening a brewery. At one point in his architectural engineering career, Pat was not finding his position rewarding. Homebrewing became an outlet for him. Pat developed a love for brewing, becoming obsessed with the science behind it during those lost evenings. His obsession led him to the Johnson County Brewing Society, which broadened the playing field for him as he had the opportunity to meet two local brewers he watched open small-scale brewery taprooms (Sandhills Brewery in Mission and Limitless Brewing in Lenexa) on the Johnson County Ale Trail.

Pat and Heather's beer started catching the attention of craft beer fans at events, including the KC Nanobrew Festival and Blarney Brew Off. Pat continued to push his craft, taking in all feedback to further improve his brewing capabilities. He is one of a handful of brewers across the state who also are certified beer judges (from the Beer Judge Certification Program, or BJCP). Knowledge gained through feedback from other judges led to further improvements to his beer, increasing Pat's confidence that the time was nearing to go pro.

The idea of opening a brewery grew from a dream to reality as they developed a plan and looked for a home. They opened Lost Evenings

Lost Evenings Brewing Company. *Courtesy of Lost Evenings Brewing Company, Lenexa, Kansas.*

Brewing Company in Lenexa during the first year of the pandemic. Since opening, the couple has had to persevere, redefining themselves as the landscape changed, and customer behaviors vacillated based on the severity of COVID.

Lost Evenings has space for its customers to relax in and is a family-friendly brewery. Heather and Pat focus on creating a welcoming environment, where we can appreciate his great beer. Beer fans will find eight tap options, with weekly introductions of a fresh style as they rotate beer styles. Pat leans into American and English styles, adding a twist to his recipes, which will keep you coming back. Music fans will connect viscerally with the beer through the music-inspired naming of the styles. This brewery is a must stop as you enjoy exploring the Ale Trail through Johnson County.

8. LIMITLESS BREWING

9765 Widmer Road * Lenexa, KS 66215
9500 Dice Lane * Lenexa, Kansas 66215 (Fall 2022 opening at new
   location)
913-526-3258
limitlessbrewing.com/index.html
www.facebook.com/limitlessbrew
Brewing System: 10BBL

Authoring this book has come with its roadblocks. My visit to Limitless was the first in close to ten days as I recovered from a herniated disc injury. Getting back into the saddle at Limitless Brewing was fitting, as I put a framework around my physical limitations. I met Dave and Emily Mobley, owners of Limitless, which is the largest brewery with the highest production capacity within the JoCo Ale Trail community. They told me that with the naming of their brewery, they "refused to be defined" as they started working to open Limitless. To Dave and Emily, the naming was a rallying cry for everyone that we all can step outside of ourselves. Emily mentioned that "so many people put parameters on themselves based on what other people think you can do."[16]

I applaud this couple and love how ingrained they have become with their community. On the last Sunday of every month, they hold an event called "Sunday with a Pourpose," donating two dollars of every pour to a local

Time for a pint at Limitless Brewing. *Courtesy of Limitless Brewing, Lenexa, Kansas.*

nonprofit organization. The support has touched multiple organizations and is community-driven, with Limitless customers often suggesting who they could help.

The brewery will be relocating in 2022 near West 95th Street and Dice Lane, down the street from its original location. Dave and Emily are excited about the potential with the new space. Relocating would not have been possible if it were not for their community of supporters. Production capability will increase to keep up with the beer demand as their community spends time together in new spaces such as the large outdoor seating area in their design plans. "We're excited to be staying in Lenexa and being able to grow," Emily shared, going on to say, "We started with nothing, and to be able to grow to this, I'm just really excited about it."[17]

They wrote a beer blog for about a year, falling in love with breweries and the community feeling they create. The two traveled the country, meeting brewery owners who had just opened or were on the journey toward realizing their dream. Dave and Emily were inspired by the people they met, realizing that their dream was possible. Despite not having any homebrewing experience, research about the brewery industry drove their desire to open a brewery and then learn how to brew. During the first year, Dave worked with and learned about the brewery process with two brewers.

Limitless Brewing is a low-key, come-as-you-are neighborhood brewery. Most of its customers live within a three-mile radius. Dave's brewing approach has evolved since opening. At first, they tried to do everything, pouring from twelve taps. They now serve ten styles ranging from a lager to stouts, sours and their bestselling IPA styles. The two love how they have created a community gathering spot, hosting everything from one-year-old birthday parties to wedding anniversary celebrations. As the name implies, Limitless's future is full of potential as the brewery next door that people want to come back to.

9. RED CROW BREWING COMPANY

1062 West Santa Fe Street * Olathe, Kansas 66061
913-247-3641
redcrowbrew.com
www.facebook.com/RedCrowBrewingCompany
Brewing System: 7BBL

"When we first opened, there were no grain to glass breweries in Johnson County,"[18] Misty said, sitting next to her husband, Chris Roberts. The brewery had originally opened in Spring Hill in 2015. Four years later, Red Crow relocated to its new home in Olathe. The couple proudly looks back, knowing that their efforts to open their brewery created a positive change in Johnson County, which has been instrumental in the craft brewery growth. Chris talked about how great it is to know that "[w]e became the litmus test for others that were considering opening."[19] The warmth that I felt in their company exemplifies how supportive and helpful they have been with the owners of breweries scattered along the Johnson County Ale Trail.

My in-law, Kevin, and I were on our second stop on a three-brewery day trip. We walked into the space on the eve of a Kansas snowstorm, escaping the cold in which Mother Nature had wrapped us. The couple met at Fort Hays State and started brewing together out of garage space. As the beer got better, the family gatherings became more frequent. Chris was recognized early in his brewing career with awards for two styles that can still be found on tap at Red Crow: the Isabelle Belgian Blonde and Elaine Rye Porter.

Chris has an assistant on board who can gain experience from a head brewer who has a wealth of knowledge, a passion for ingredients and a

Look for Clancy the Crow at Red Crow Brewing Company. *Courtesy of Red Crow Brewing Company, Olathe, Kansas.*

curiosity to dissect recipes and find ways to make styles uniquely his. The brewhouse vessels are named after famous artists, which is fitting, as the brew team brings artistry to each pint poured through the tap list of ten styles. Chris shared the story behind the naming of his vessels, highlighting a high school art teacher who was influential in his youth. Their brewhouse is focused on brewing what their demographic likes, which today leans toward a malt-forward crowd.

Patrons will typically find at least one of the owners at the brewery, ready to welcome them as one would a parent, brother or sister. Misty manages the front of the house with an energy and passion that customers can immediately feel. She talked about how intimidating it was years ago to walk into a brewery, afraid to say anything because she felt so out of place. Those memories have shaped Misty's approach with the staff, who immediately make you feel welcomed. The experience quickly becomes memorable and relaxed as that first pint is placed in front of you.

Family has a presence in the brewery every day. When the two walk in and see Clancy the Crow, the iconic image in their logo, they remember the long lists of brewery names that Chris kept generating. Misty remembers the day that Red Crow Brewing was on a list, immediately visualizing how Red

Crow would look. The family unanimously embraced Red Crow, a name with no deep personal meaning at first, and it has evolved into a brewery watched over by Clancy as he proudly sees his granddaughter living a dream come true.

Customers sit at the bar and ask for beer styles that all have women's names. They connect with their favorite beers and are eager to share with new customers that Donna is named after Chris's grandmother and that Bev is named after Misty's crazy-cool aunt. Next time, ask for the story behind Margaret, Mary and Anne. All craft beer fans who like to experiment need to immediately check out styles on the board named Sybil. The couple thought it would be fitting to use the name of a woman who was the billboard for multiple personality disorders to capture the test styles that have evolved from Sybil-1 to Sybil-23 at the time I wrote this profile.

Red Crow is a must stop on the Ale Trail. The brewery was the first to open in Johnson County and has the largest space of any along the trail. Come on a warm summer day and you will not want to leave the big patio or inside space, which transforms into outside space as the six garage doors are rolled up. It will not take long for you to spot Clancy. Misty shared that she likes "thinking that he is always here."[20]

10. TALL TRELLIS BREW CO

25600 West Valley Parkway * Olathe, Kansas 66061
913-249-5077
talltrellis.com
www.facebook.com/talltrellis
Brewing System: 1BBL

Tall Trellis has more to offer than the typical brewery in Kansas—think taproom, coffeehouse, nanobrewery and Kansas hopyard all in one shared space. Imagine a large patio, yard games, event space and green space. The innovators behind this endeavor are two guys with wives who are sisters, both couples raising three children. Ryan Triggs and Nick Feightner, co-owners, are excited about their brewery serving as an educational tool. Ryan sees the experience awaiting you as "kind of like a vineyard type deal,"[21] where you can appreciate the process from the ground the hops grow on to the glass that becomes home to a fresh pint of wet hop beer brewed

Check out Tall Trellis Brew Co. Ryan and Nick have hops growing just off the patio. *Courtesy of Tall Trellis Brew Co, Olathe, Kansas.*

on site. "Everyone needs to experience this," Ryan went on to say. "It is a sense of place where people are going to be able to experience something that is only possible in a few places in the world."[22]

Ryan and Nick, who also own Kansas Hop Company[23] in Ottawa with one other partner, envision hopyard tours and the chance to share knowledge about the different varieties of hops that are used in brewing. After your hopyard tour, step into the taproom and enjoy the opportunity to select a pint from sixteen options. Tall Trellis offers twelve guest taps with a diverse style selection highlighting breweries from the region. Its goal is to try to rotate as many breweries as possible that are Kansas Hop Company customers through the taps with something for everybody. Ryan said, "We love hoppy beers; obviously we are hop farmers too!"[24] The other four taps have small-batch beer crafted by the two in their one-barrel brewhouse. This is the only brewery in the state—and one of few in the country—where the brewers can pick hops that are just feet away, throwing them directly in the kettle.

The hopyard, with twenty-two-foot Nebraska yellow pine poles, has Cascade hop bines growing up to seven months a year. The team has created space between the rows of bines for families to have dinner and couples to hang out with a pint in the shade created by the hop bines and host magical wedding ceremonies. Tall Trellis is in town, but when you pull into the parking lot, it will feel like you have stepped onto a farm. Looking at a wall of hop bines that stretches one hundred feet across will no doubt be memorable. Count on Tall Trellis Brew Co to host its first annual fresh hop harvest festival in the fall of 2022.

These guys defied logic once, becoming successful hop farmers in Kansas of all places, learning how to grow eight varieties of hops supplied to breweries across the Midwest. As Nick talked about this, I saw the parallel with what he and Ryan are creating at Tall Trellis, once again challenging logic. Growing hops has been a success for the team, who decided that the next venture would be Tall Trellis versus expanding farm hop acreage. Nick noted, "The farm has allowed us to do this."[25]

One of the coolest things I learned from the team is that their beers brewed on site will often be collaboration beers. The community of breweries that supported the hop company will be highlighted across the guest taps as a way of saying thanks. When brewers stop in to pick up their hops, Ryan and Nick will invite them to hang out for a brew day. The four taps highlighting their beer will often have collaboration brews that will only be available just a short distance from great patio space and the hopyard. Tall Trellis is ready to offer you unique experiences that are not matched by any brewery across our state.

11. EXBEERIMENT BREWING

925 East Lincoln Lane * Gardner, Kansas 66030
913-938-4175
www.exbeerimentbrewing.com
www.facebook.com/ExBEERimentBrewing
Brewing System: 3½BBL

"It is an experiment for us owning a business for the first time,"[26] Misty shared as we discussed the journey that she and her husband, Greg Eytcheson, have had in their first year as owners. ExBEERiment Brewing is a child of the pandemic. Life became challenging for Misty and Greg when the pandemic affected their lives, as we all have experienced. In a world of negatives and stress, the two sought positives and promise through discussing what was their next life chapter. As the conversation continued, the idea of opening a brewery took shape.

They and their twin daughters are Gardner residents in a growing community that previously did not have a brewery. Their taproom became real in the spring of 2021. The two have backgrounds that are complementary. Greg brings an IT background to the brewery coupled with more than ten years of homebrewing experience. Misty's last job was as director of communication for the Spring Hill School District. Her strong marketing and people skills background is a great match for their brewery.

The brewery name ExBEERiment celebrates this experiment that has been well received, with a loyal community of supporters growing. Greg loves the process and creativity in brewing. His focus stylistically starts and ends with motivation to brew what he likes. Two of their styles have become core favorites, including their Validation cream ale, which is the choice for a new customer who gravitates to the commercial light lagers such as Bud Light. The Hypothesis Hazy IPA hones in on their long conversations and shared hypothesis that there was clearly white space for the town's first brewery. As our style conversation continued, I learned about tomato beer, a favorite in the southeastern Kansas rural town where Misty grew up. "Tomato beers were a thing."[27] In a way, the team pays homage to this creative option through their Red Beer style. Greg will continue to round out the twelve tap options with seasonal and creative styles to complement the two core beers.

ExBEERiment is on the Ale Trail, holding the farthest position south. The spirit and enthusiastic sense of humor that you will see and feel when visiting is wonderful. The experiment for them can also be the same for customers who step up to the bar and say, "I don't like IPAs." Misty warmly said that she enjoys building a bridge for customers to experiment at ExBEERiment. Her response to the customer who isn't a fan of IPAs is, "Do you like citrus flavors? Try this."[28]

12. OUTFIELD BEER COMPANY

Olde Mill Building, 611 West 2nd Street * Bonner Springs, Kansas 66012
913-276-0142
www.outfieldbeer.com
Brewing System: 5BBL

"When I was ten, my baseball career was over,"[29] Beau Martin shared. Beau, owner and head brewer, loves the national pastime. Outfield Beer Company offers baseball fans a memorable experience, including baseball-themed beer names to tabletops that have baseball cards embedded in them. My son-in-law, Chris, and I were nostalgic looking at the memorabilia. The name Outfield Beer Company came to be through the fusion of Beau's love for baseball and the farm fields that his brother-in-law, Greg Bush, works.

Since our first visit, Beau and Jason Weiser (owner and brewmaster at Own Agenda, which opened in 2021) decided to merge the two breweries and establish a home in the Olde Mill Building for the new Outfield Beer Company. The space is unique, reminding me of the building in the movie *Footloose*, where the kids danced despite the resistance from the older generation in the fictitious town of Beaumont. The brewery carries the

Outfield Beer Company. *Courtesy of Outfield Beer Company, Bonner Springs, Kansas.*

same elements from Beau's original space, enhanced by the partnership with Jason, who retired after serving in the army for more than twenty-five years and six deployments. Jason, who loves to brew, was able to pursue his passion after retiring with honor from the military.

Beau, a Kansas State graduate with a degree in foods and nutrition, has had an interesting path from home plate to first base. A new job for his wife took them to Toledo, presenting him with an opportunity to change careers, leaving behind a clinical nutrition position. He walked into Toledo's original craft brewery with a résumé in hand and found himself employed moments later. He launched his professional brewing career with Maumee Bay Brewing Company. He had the opportunity to work with a fifteen-barrel copper brewhouse, honing his craft as part of a two-man brewing team.

Beau went back to school while brewing, getting a nursing degree like his mom, and stepped into a world of serving and caring for others. The family moved back to Kansas to be closer to his mom, whose health was failing. Beau is now a school nurse at the elementary school that his children attend, as well as co-owner of Outfield Beer Company.

Beau and Jason brew a lineup of ten handcrafted beers, rotating seasonal options in and honoring beer traditions and German styling. Beau's approach, focusing on refreshing, hoppy and roasted malt styles, will evolve as he and Jason blend their talents together. As I wrapped up the experience of tasting his lineup, Beau said, "You never know what tomorrow will bring."[30] That rings so true for Beau and Outfield Beer Company as the next chapter takes shape in 2022. Check out the magic Beau and Jason are creating. Know that Beau wants his space to be a home where he can serve old and new friends, a place thirsty for conversations in a crowd of patrons looking to quench their thirst with a pint. Beau knows!

13. RANGE 23 BREWING

Due West Ranch, 13400 Donahoo Road, Building B * Kansas City,
    Kansas 66109
913-229-0992
www.range23brewing.com
www.facebook.com/range23brewing
Brewing System: 1BBL

Driving to Range 23 Brewing takes you through captivating rolling hills as you head north on Route 7 toward Due West Ranch. As Nate and Karen Schotanus playfully warn you on their website, watch for the carefree dogs, horses, occasional goat and kids as you drive down the long gravel road before pulling up next the ranch's event space where the brewery is located.

Nate and Karen are not only the parents of two daughters, Holly and Penelope, but also busy professionals. Karen is a freelance communications professional, running her writing and editing business from home. Nate is a firefighter for the city of Kansas City, Kansas. He fell in love with firefighting and serving his community, helping people in need as a paramedic as well. The two have taken a similar approach with their brewery, this time motivated by the desire to serve as an impetus to attract more small businesses to open in western Wyandotte County.

As their married life unfolded, Nate developed a talent at homebrewing, which was validated through testimonial from family and friends. The couple knew that, as their girls grew older, the idea of opening a small business could be a possibility. When they moved into the Piper School District and made this community their home, they were struck by the independent restaurant, coffee shop and brewery desert. Discussions about opening a coffee shop were sidelined due to the higher cost outlay and logistical hurdles to make it happen. They knew that Nate was a talented homebrewer and started

Take a seat outside Range 23 Brewing. *Courtesy of Range 23 Brewing, Kansas City, Kansas.*

thinking that scaling up slightly from his current setup would be more cost effective and a better fit with their family schedule.

Karen was volunteering for the nonprofit therapeutic riding center located at Due West Ranch on Donahoo Road. Karma struck during a conversation with the ranch owners when they suggested that the young couple consider using the kitchen area of the event space for their brewery. Karen told me they thought, "Maybe this is the opportunity that we've been looking at for decades. Now we've found that place that needs it. Let's figure it out."[31]

Range 23 Brewing opened in May 2020. Nate's strategy is to always have six core beers available, mixing in seasonally appropriate styles. The day I visited, Holly was hard at work helping her dad with the canning of one of the fresh-squeezed craft soda options. The couple is committed to offering something for anyone who visits, from a good craft beer to a quality cup of coffee.

The naming of the brewery is linked to the U.S. Public Land Survey System (PLSS),[32] which I knew little about when I pulled into the brewery. The system, which was established after the Revolutionary War, was a way to legally describe and record parcels of land. Two of our founding fathers, Thomas Jefferson and John Adams, led a political movement that brought PLSS to life. They vehemently argued that wealthy men and land speculation companies did not have the right to control all the land. Township parcels were created, and then a smaller parcel size within those townships, ranges, were established. Range 23 Brewing is located within section 19, township 10, range 23. Most of the Piper community is located within this range.

Karen and Nate felt it was important that their name reflect the community that they serve. They are focused on community and creating an inclusive space for families and craft beer fans to visit. Do not blink twice because you could easily miss the eight-hour window that they are typically open several days per week. Follow Range 23 on Facebook, Instagram and Twitter; Karen does a wonderful job of posting about events, parties and new beer offerings, which no doubt will give you the excuse to go for a nice drive. Just remember, watch out for the dogs, the farm equipment and their daughters!

Steve Nicholson at his Center Pivot Restaurant & Brewery in Quinter, Kansas. *Author's collection.*

Chapter 7

THE LITTLE BREWERY
THAT COULD

Mill, mill, mill. Mash, mash, mash. Boil, boil, boil. Crash, crash, crash. Ferment, ferment, ferment.

Center Pivot in Quinter, Kansas, was a single-barrel brewery. Barrel limitations did not prevent the brewer from turning out interesting beer styles with a twist. There were five beer styles, including ales with cracked pepper, green tea and even a brown ale named after Maizee, one of the brewer's dogs. Rounding out the five styles were the Taw-Taw pomegranate wheat and the Main Street IPA.

But that was not all. There was a brewer, eighty-one inches tall. Steve was his name, teaching and brewing great craft beer were part of his game. In this little brewery in Quinter, Steve almost did not brew. This is the story, and it is true.

Steve Nicholson lived in Nebraska for years. This is where he met his wife, Ericka, who one day would become a bookkeeper for the little brewery. Teaching was his claim to fame, and coaching was his sport of choice. There came a point when Steve and his friends tired of drinking Michelob Amber Bock and Fat Tire. He and a coaching friend decided one day to start homebrewing. Close to twenty years later, Steve dreamed of opening a brewery in Nebraska. He continued to brew at home, refining his processes and experimenting with taste profiles. He pursued the possibilities but was unable to secure a home for his dream. Steve the brewer looked south and found a new place to teach and, best of all, a potential home for the little brewery. Main Street in Quinter lacked a sit-down restaurant and gathering place for the community. Steve said, "I want to build a place for families and large groups to come, be together and socialize."[1]

> The homebrewer and aspiring pro brewer thought to himself:
> "Open in Quinter? I homebrew for my friends but have a
> mountain to climb. The town is dry, I cry!"

Steve respected the German heritage and diverse beliefs in the Quinter area. The challenge was to convince the Dunkard Brethren community that his dream of creating a space for everyone could work in this town of 911 people.

> Debate was contentious; libations were not welcome.

Steve and the team behind Center Pivot found a way to create a space that was comfortable for everyone, with the dining room and brewery clearly separated. The greater Quinter community immediately pitched in to help. Newfound friends joined hands collectively, as they helped raise the roof of Center Pivot Restaurant & Brewery.

> The calendar months fell away; close to forty-eight pages fell
> in a fray.

"We can make this happen,"[2] Steve declared. He approached the space with an Americana flair, recycling materials and incorporating contributions from the community into the design. Doors, chairs, walls and halls came together with the help of new friends and neighbors. Local artists delivered Center Pivot coasters made from old hedge posts, a brewery farmers' lounge came to life through use of a retired truck tailgate, and beer flight trays were made from expired license plates.

> Opening day neared; will they like my beer, he feared.

Comically, at the grand opening, Steve thought that the kegs of beer "must be leaking" because they drained so quickly. His beer was a hit! Steve reminisced, "Some of my ideas for beer styles have been a little ahead of the curve. I want my beer styles to be drinkable. The taste should be just enough to get your attention, but not a punch in the head."[3]

> He boiled, fermented, filtered and slowly, slowly, slowly, the brews hit the taps.

Steve has accomplished this transition from homebrewing to pro, with a used one-barrel system that Copper Kettle Brewing Company in Denver had outgrown. He has continued to introduce styles with unique flavor notes to his followers. A winter beer, appropriately named Spruce Is Loose, has hit the mark with the timely use of spruce tips and Norwegian old-style brewing techniques. Outside-the-box thinking prompted by a friend making a kind of Kahlúa has resulted in a stout style called Veracruz, loaded with local coffee and Kahlúa. If you become a regular at Center Pivot, know that your taste buds will be happy as new styles rotate through.

> And the little brewery, named Center Pivot, you see…named after an irrigation system that pivots, creating crop circles within squares that a soaring hawk can see from up high while flying over Main Street.

As you visit the eight breweries in the "Smoky Hill Trail"[4] chapter that follows, enjoy the three breweries that opened in 2021 in rural towns from Phillipsburg to Courtland. The 148-mile trek west on Kansas I-70 will end as you slow down, taking Exit 107 to Quinter. Pass the flower display in the vintage milk can straddling the center of Main Street and discover the little brewery with great beer down on the right. Walk in and Steve will greet you like a long-lost friend.

> "All I want is for you to ask for a second pint."[5]

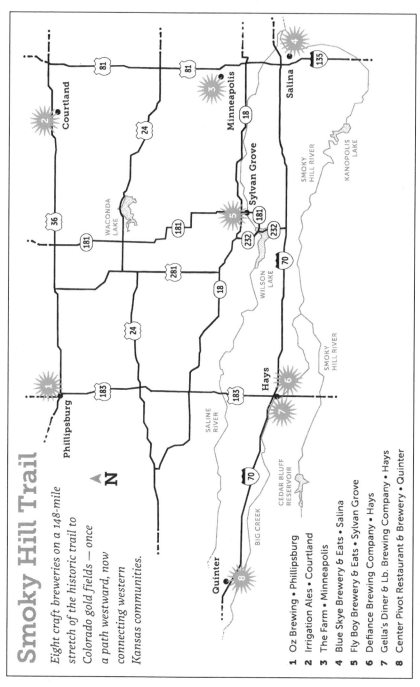

Smoky Hill Trail

Eight craft breweries on a 148-mile stretch of the historic trail to Colorado gold fields — once a path westward, now connecting western Kansas communities.

1 Oz Brewing • Phillipsburg
2 Irrigation Ales • Courtland
3 The Farm • Minneapolis
4 Blue Skye Brewery & Eats • Salina
5 Fly Boy Brewery & Eats • Sylvan Grove
6 Defiance Brewing Company • Hays
7 Gella's Diner & Lb. Brewing Company • Hays
8 Center Pivot Restaurant & Brewery • Quinter

Smoky Hill Trail map. *Courtesy of Christy Schneider, Inkello Design & Letterpress, East Lawrence, Kansas.*

Chapter 8

SMOKY HILL TRAIL

1. OZ BREWING

603 4th Street * Phillipsburg, Kansas 67661
785-208-0065
www.ozbrewing.com
m.facebook.com/ozbrewing
Brewing System: 3BBL

Six blocks from Matt's childhood home was a creepy old brick building on the corner of 4th Street. Matt's imagination often ran wild as he walked by this building, hesitating as he looked toward the front door that was ajar. It was less than inviting.

Moving forward in time to 2018, Matt and his wife, Stephanie, had decided to move back to his hometown from Colorado. They were looking for a home and kept driving by the very same brick building that had a "For Sale" sign in front of it. The last time they looked at this former Masonic building, their vision took shape, propelled by their engineering and design backgrounds. Stephanie mentioned that they took ownership of what could have been a haunted house!

Three years later, they had completely redone the two floors, building a New York–style loft for themselves upstairs while creating a welcoming, cool space for craft beer fans on the main floor. The two had traveled extensively

Oz Brewing in a restored former Masonic building. *Courtesy of Oz Brewing, Phillipsburg, Kansas.*

while both were immersed in their professions and studied breweries, their spaces and vibe as they dreamed about opening their own. Oz Brewing in Phillipsburg is one of the most striking breweries in Kansas. One descriptive word, *twist*, comes to mind when I think about how they have built out this new space, including a full kitchen, in a town of fewer than 2,500 citizens. The homage to the *Wizard of Oz* shines through in their approach to all their design and experience features. The Oz theme is evident throughout the space from your table to the tap handles.

Of course, everything starts with the beer. Matt and Stephanie met in Colorado, found a shared passion for craft beer and spent time homebrewing together. The style approach they have taken starts with offering wheat beer with a twist, incorporating unique flavors into the base. Their commercial light beer fans have transitioned to craft beer through this style. Across the board, you will find a presence of IPAs, a hefeweizen and seasonal beers including porters, which are a favorite of Stephanie's. Trust me, you will not leave thirsty.

I met these two back in August, two months before they officially opened their doors. They have big hopes for expansion and new ventures with the brewery. Their full kitchen menu will highlight smoked meats from their monstrous smoker out back. The spirit and passion they have for this community gathering spot is contagious. Their fans love the beautiful space, bringing a local spirit to the brewery owned by a neighbor who has finally come home. I promise that if you visit once, you will be back!

2. IRRIGATION ALES

414 Main Street * Courtland, Kansas 66939
irrigationales.com
www.facebook.com/irrigationales
Brewing System: 3BBL

"Rural matters, rural has value."[1] Luke and Jennifer Mahin are proud to tell anyone that they are rural by choice. The couple, who are co-owners of Irrigation Ales in Courtland, took different journeys before embracing their shared rural life. Luke, who grew up three blocks from the brewery, opted to come home after finishing his degree at Fort Hays State. Jennifer, who grew up in Pennsylvania, decided to try something different, transferring to the University of Nebraska–Kearney for her senior year.

Her friends thought she was crazy when she moved to Courtland, establishing her roots with her new husband, Luke, in a town of three hundred folks. Jennifer shared that she loves the people and the quality of life and could not imagine living somewhere else. This couple is one of a small group of entrepreneurs who have come "home," intent on having a simpler yet richer life, while opening wonderful breweries in rural Kansas towns.

Irrigation Ales, owned by Luke and Jennifer Mahin. *Courtesy of Irrigation Ales, Courtland, Kansas.*

Luke, the economic development director for Republic County, introduced me to Marci Penner, co-founder and executive director of the Kansas Sampler Foundation. Her nonprofit organization believes in rural culture, community and our beloved state of Kansas. One of the principal missions that resulted from her organization's Kansas Power Up & Go project[2] is supporting civic champions, entrepreneurs, public servants and volunteers by creating a place that everyone is proud to call home. Her passion for the state and young entrepreneurs rang true in 2021, when she brought three brewery ownership groups together that were opening in rural Kansas towns, including the Ladybird Brewing duo, the Riverbank Brewing team and the Mahins. Luke celebrates the fact that he can reach out to these teams whenever he has questions, gaining new insights from the two breweries that opened in the late fall of 2021.

That spirit of community that Marci is renowned for, strengthening and celebrating our state, is alive in the sleepy, small town of Courtland. While Luke makes great strides with county development, Jennifer is doing amazing things as a teacher specializing in STEM education (science, technology, engineering and math), creating the opportunity for all K-5 students in her school system to have access to this education. In their "free time," they opened Irrigation Ales.

Irrigation Ales is a taproom offering six taps to beer fans, while offering snacks and appetizers as well. Luke brings more than a decade of award-winning homebrewing skills to customers at the brewery. The couple's intent is to offer four core beers to appeal to all, while pushing experimentation and adventure through two taps dedicated to testing our palates.

Courtland is a town with a progressive approach to development and creating a community spirit. Luke mentioned that there are more than thirty-five businesses in town that serve people from as far away as an hour's drive. He has historically been a key planner behind Courtland Fun Day, an annual summer celebration held the last Saturday in July for fifty-seven years and counting. People will travel for beer and a chance to relax in a brewery community just as they will for the town celebration, which can bring in up to five thousand people. No doubt the Saturday beer garden will be celebrating the arrival of the town's brewery.

Luke and Jennifer are proud of where they live and honor the Kansas Bostwick Irrigation District canal system[3] through the naming of their brewery. The canal system, which irrigates more than 42,500 acres of Kansas farmland, came into existence after the area suffered through major flooding in the 1930s. When visiting the couple and enjoying a pint, look at the murals in the taproom that reflect the source and paths of the irrigation canals.

"No one can copy our sense of place," Luke said moments before the two took me for a dusk drive along a portion of one hundred miles of canals. "In the future, I would love to do tours, taking people up to the lake and touring the irrigation district."[4] Jennifer built on her husband's comments, saying, "We want to stay true to what our values are, bringing in local produce, local ingredients and sharing our story."[5]

3. THE FARM & THE ODD FELLOWS

205 West 2nd Street * Minneapolis, Kansas 67467
785-392-6614
thefarmminneapolis.com
www.facebook.com/thefarmandtheoddfellows
Brewing System: 5BBL

"We want to leave the town in a better place,"[6] shared Ashley Swisher, co-owner of The Farm with her husband, Keir, at the outset of our first conversation. Their vision started with their purchase of this historic building, constructed in 1916, which served as a lodge for members of the Odd Fellows local order. The visit that clinched it for Ashley and Keir included a mesmerizing moment as they opened doors to a grand meeting room on the second floor that had been closed for more than forty-five years. Everything fell in place for the two, who were intent on building a communal space that would become part of the heartbeat of Minneapolis.

The Swishers' vision for The Farm is to provide unique opportunities to create experiences that will foster a sense of community through different venues, including The Bean (coffee café), The Pickle (pickleball court and event space), The Seed (activity center and event space) and The Hops (brewpub and event space), with more to come. Make Minneapolis your Saturday destination and know that you could spend a full day in one building, shifting from enjoying a coffee and pastry to an hour of bowling, followed by a family foosball tournament, which could spill into an afternoon upstairs in the brew pub thirsty for a good beer and time with friends and family.

The Hops is one of the most unique brewery spaces in the state. You can walk upstairs to enjoy the brew pub, stepping into a large communal space

Check out The Farm and its venues in Minneapolis, Kansas, including the Hops Brewery and The Bean coffee café. *Author's collection.*

that feels like a vintage ballroom with décor taking you back to the good old days in America. Options unfold from sitting at communal tables to relaxing in a private living room space. The back wall is home to another first of its kind in the Sunflower State. Kyle Banman, head brewer at The Hops, is busy brewing, feeding his fourteen brite tanks beer styles that are waiting for you to pour at a self-serve tap wall!

I had the opportunity to watch this vision progress over the last year. Kyle, whom Ashley and Keir brought on board as head brewer, spent more than half a year developing recipes, brewing small batches for community events and agonizing over the significant shipping delays of their brewhouse equipment. Santa came through, delivering the ABE brewhouse and HLT (hot liquor tank) days before Christmas 2021 in a large stocking. Within months, he anticipated seeing the four fermenters and fourteen brite tanks getting delivered to the second-floor brewery.

Kyle's approach to brewing is to serve classic styles with a twist. I had the good fortune of tasting a range of beers that will be on the tap wall, including a rosemary rye IPA, a white stout, an amber ale, a hoppy brown ale and a farmhouse fig ale. Kyle has an AmeriCorps teaching background, has mentored homebrewers and is currently coach of a McPherson junior swim club.

His goal with The Hops and the brewhouse is twofold. His approach is focused on sharing the experience with their patrons, expressing his love of the craft through a range of interesting taste profiles. Kyle said, "It's been my experience that the beer turns out better that way."[7] He is excited about the second goal, hoping to create three brewing experiences, sharing the brewing environment on brew days with craft beer fans. He wants to offer half-day classes focused on the brewing process and a full brew day experience, concluding with a package that will encompass the entire brewing process from building a recipe to a tap takeover. Kyle happily informed me in early April that the brewhouse was up and running, sending me an image of him working with the mash.

Ashley and Keir met at Bethany College in Lindsborg, advancing their education and culminating in both landing roles in healthcare. Ashley owns a dental practice next door to The Farm, while Keir is an ER doctor and former chief of staff at Salina Regional Health Center.

As you walk into The Hops, look up at the ceiling. The tile ceiling is original, and the symbol on each tile speaks to tenets of the Odd Fellows organization: friendship, love and truth. The fusion of Odd Fellows social goals and the vision of Ashley and Keir are creating a perfect symphony. The couple, who have two boys, want to make the world a better place for the young kids of Minneapolis, creating an environment that fosters activities and events that can benefit the community beyond the four walls of their building. Keir told me on a later visit, as we were tasting styles, that ultimately, "Drinking beer is about the experience."[8]

4. BLUE SKYE BREWERY & EATS

116 North Santa Fe Avenue * Salina, Kansas 67401
785-404-2159
www.facebook.com/blueskyebrewery
Brewing System: 7BBL

I have had the opportunity to enjoy Blue Skye a handful of times since starting this book project. I guarantee that when you walk into the brewery, the vibrancy, happy sounds and Cheers-like environment will pull you in. Step up to the bar and discover that the bartenders know all the regulars and are quick to pour the right pint without guidance. I am not surprised that 2021 was the fourth year in a row that Salina has recognized this brewery and its team as the "Best All-Around Restaurant" in the city.

Monte Shadwick, a former Salina mayor, initiated the idea to open a brewery in downtown. There was potential that Blue Skye could be a cog in the revitalization efforts in the Salina Historic District. Destiny struck when Shadwick started asking around about homebrewers in the area. There were two firefighters who had developed a great reputation since the early 2000s

Blue Sky Brewery & Eats, owned by firefighters, brewing good craft beer. *Courtesy of Blue Sky Brewery, Salina, Kansas.*

for their talents. John Goertzen and Josh Foley, immersed in homebrewing, had started a brew club back in 2005. Ironically, John's sister-in-law worked for Monte Shadwick. The bridge to these brewers was built as she connected them with Monte.

Fire Station No. 1 in Salina is the headquarters as well as home to the two firefighters, who homebrewed together for more than a decade before Monte approached them. Conversations evolved, and the two realized that they could make a brewery work by brewing during off-hours, serving the community in a unique way.

Expect a great lineup of core beer styles, including the Fire Engine Red, which pays homage to their firefighter brethren. The brewers rotate seasonal and new styles to round out the options. The vibrancy is fueled by great wood-fired pizza. This brewery does a wonderful job of introducing craft beer to patrons through traditional styles.

I must give special recognition to the firefighters in Salina, KCK and Coffeyville who are owners and/or brewers at three Kansas breweries. Firefighters, as they serve our communities, are close-knit families, bonded through the risks they take every day.

Josh was quoted as saying, "John and I are both real dedicated firefighters, but we tell some of our best friends [that] these are the best two jobs in the world, so we couldn't be much happier."

5. FLY BOY BREWERY & EATS

105 North Main Street * Sylvan Grove, Kansas 67481
785-526-7800
www.facebook.com/flyboybreweryandeats
Brewing System: 3BBL

"It feels good to provide a place for people to spend time with those that they love. Hearing this place roar is absolutely enthralling. It kind of gives you a jolt,"[9] said Lucas Hass, co-owner and brewer at Fly Boy Brewery & Eats. Earlier, I had stood on Main Street and reflected that I was in the smallest rural Kansas town to have a neighborhood brewery. Population counts back in 2010 show that 295 citizens called the Grove home. Today, the population hovers around 257 citizens.

Lucas, with co-owner and chef Grant Wagner, bought the business from the original owners in January 2021. I have a newfound appreciation after my visit for the fusion of the history of the brewery with the 2021 refinements. Grant is the bridge between the past and future, having served as the inaugural chef for the Harings, who opened Fly Boys in 2014. He has come back to Fly Boy, bringing his Arizona culinary education and skills to the community. The walls are still decorated with photographs of planes that Clay Haring either owned or built during the days when he was an agricultural spray pilot and brewery owner.

Little did I know as my in-law, Kevin, drove us past vistas of sylvan charm on the way into town that five miles to the west was Wilson Lake and its historic hotel, the Midland Railroad Hotel. Lake traffic coming in on the Post Rock Scenic byway brings quite a bit of business to the team at Fly Boy during the summer months. For those considering making a trip out this way, consider booking one of twenty-eight rooms at the Midland to spend the night in after enjoying a delicious dinner with a pint or two at Fly Boy.

Think of the history in the brewery, including the ninety-three years it was a hardware store. The second floor was at one point a Freemason Lodge, a basketball court and a destination for Ford Model Ts that were brought upstairs on a grain elevator. Step into the Midland, built in 1899, surrounded by the history and glamour that one of the finest Midwest hotels offered the Union Pacific Railroad travelers moving between Kansas City and Denver. During the Depression, the owners raised chickens on the third floor to feed their guests. The three-story limestone hotel will remind you of the limestone buildings on Main Street that once were homes to thriving businesses.

Experience the great food and beer at Fly Boy Brewery & Eats. *Courtesy of Fly Boy Brewery, Sylvan Grove, Kansas.*

Lucas and Grant are carrying the torch forward into 2022, pleased with the momentum they built in their first year of ownership. The brewery thrives, giving high schoolers in the county an opportunity to work, make money and be part of the Fly Boy family. Lucas watched a young waiter, Hunter, connecting with the full tables and said, "It is tough to think about some of them leaving this year."[10] The environment created is compelling enough that Hunter has committed to coming back from Fort Hays State University on weekends to still be a part of the family.

The brewery offers eight styles on tap, with Lucas continuing to brew all the original recipes. Lucas is brewing experimental batches of German-inspired styles, for which he has a passion. I have inside knowledge that one of his favorite beers is the KC Bier Company Dunkel. A Fly Boy Dunkel recipe could be fermenting in his mind!

The brewery attracts customers from Salina to Hays and everywhere between looking for a fine steak dinner or a casual burger and beer. Grant's team makes as much as they can on the menu from scratch. The brewery is open for dinners only, Thursday through Saturday. They do not take reservations, so make sure you are ready to be patient, especially if you show up on Prime Rib Weekend, when a line can spill down the street. Lucas closed by talking about a recent Saturday night, with the roar of the patrons warming his heart, saying, "It is like musical chairs in here all night long. One thing I hope never changes is the community aspect of this area."[11]

6. DEFIANCE BREWING COMPANY

2050 East Highway 40 * Hays, Kansas 67601
785-301-BEER (2337)
Defiance Brewing Company Downtown
111 West 7th Street * Hays, Kansas 67601
785-621-2730
www.defiancebeer.com
www.facebook.com/DefianceBrewingCo
www.facebook.com/Defiance-Brewing-Co-Downtown
Brewing System: 20BBL

Three synonyms for the word *defiance* are *daring*, *boldness* and *audacity*. When Matt Bender and Dylan Sultzer, co-owners of Defiance Brewing Company, decided to open their brewery in 2014, the naming of their brewery came easily. They shared that it was time to break out of the box, getting away from the expected, which had been their focus while part of the brew team at Lb. Brewing. To open a new brewery outside of downtown Hays and to focus brewing a large family of IPAs were daring and bold moves. These two young guys were defiant that an original approach could work. Guess what? It has.

Matt explained his job in simple terms: "To get Dylan's creations in as many mouths as possible."[12] Matt, the yang to Dylan's yin, is focused on managing the operations of Defiance while still occasionally getting creative in the brewhouse.

Dylan is the graphic artist, designer and head brewer. He described his brewing approach: "I think, me personally, I think it is about 100 percent

Beer	Style	ABV	4oz	8oz	16oz	32w	64w
COBBLER GOBBLER	PEACH COBBLER GOSE	4.5%	$3	$4	$6	$7/$11	$12/$11
UNION	COFFEE ALE	5%	$3	$4	$6	$7/$11	$13/$16
YOU RE MY BOY BLUE!	BLUEBERRY GOSE	4.5%	$3	$4	$6	$7/$11	$12/$16
FUZZY KNUCKLES	IMPERIAL STOUT	10%	$4	$5	X	$8/$12	$11/$20
NOWHERE IN SIGHT	PILSNER	5%	$3	$4	$6	$7/$11	$12/$16
NO BAKE	CHERRY CHEESECAKE GOSE	5%	$3	$4	$6	$7/$11	$12/$16
AWESOMENESS	HAZY DIPA	8%	$3	$4	$6	$7/$11	$12/$16
APRI-GOSE FRAGALISTIC	APRICOT GOSE	4.5%	$3	$4	$6	$7/$11	$12/$16
PROMISE LAND	HAZY IPA	7%	$3	$4	$6	$7/$11	$12/$16
BIG MONEY	BREAKFAST IPA	7%	$3	$4	$6	$7/$11	$12/$16
SPILLED THE SALT	GOSE	5%	$4	C	A	N	S
WITH FRIENDS	PALE ALE	5.8%	$4	C	A	N	S

Defiance Brewing Company beer board at its first location out on the Old 40 in Hays. *Courtesy of Defiance Brewing Company.*

more art. We have done the processes so many times, we know what works and what doesn't. I am always shooting for a flavor profile."[13] He is an artist, plain and simple. He dabbled in his early homebrewing days in barrel-aged beers.

Brewing a range of styles "keeps it fun" for Dylan. At the time I visited, he was experimenting with lagers, putting a helles on tap, working to nail down a Czech pils, while getting ready to start the barrel-aged program. Dylan said, "We are IPA focused but want to have beers for different palates."[14]

Kenny Gottschalk, co-owner with Matt and Dylan, knew that it was "Defiance time." Prior to the start of the pandemic, the team was working to open a location in Kansas City. COVID brought those plans to a stop. "The more we pulled back, the more we started growing,"[15] Matt shared. Shutting down the KC project, pulling back the number of states they had been distributing to and focusing on what put them on the map fostered positive results. Shifting the focus on expansion to their backyard led to the opening of their second location, a brewery, beer hall and pizza joint in downtown Hays. Expect a great mix of people spending time together at their 7th

Street location, enjoying beer and pizza in a boisterous space. If chilling in a taproom while having a one-on-one conversation with the bartender is what you look forward to, drive out of town to their Old Highway 40 patio oasis.

Matt and Dylan talked about approaching their business, taking measured steps one at a time and keeping their eyes on their two Hays locations. Rest assured that Matt will keep future growth like a KC location on the table. Their downtown location, home to their barrel-aged program, will produce sours that cater to a "generation that grew up on sour patch kids and warheads."[16] Dylan will continue to brew a range of beer styles for everyone, with drinkability as the endgame.

Matt and Dylan are quick to say that they have been uncomfortable since opening Defiance. To be daring, bold and different comes with its pressures. The two, backed by Kenny and other investors, have not backed down. Support Defiance, be bold with your choice of a pint and watch out for these two. Matt closed our conversation, nodding to Dylan and saying, "We have a lot of dreams and aspirations."[17]

7. GELLA'S DINER + LB. BREWING COMPANY

117 East 11th Street * Hays, Kansas 67601
785-621-2739
www.lbbrewing.com
www.facebook.com/LbBrewing
Brewing System: 10BBL

Have you ever heard of Rome, Kansas? More than likely, you will be as surprised as I was to learn that there was indeed a town called Rome. Back in the late 1860s, Rome was home to thirty-seven saloons and a brewery called Brewing Company, located on the banks of Big Creek.[18] Buffalo Bill Cody's headquarters were part of this town of two thousand souls. Think about the characters who were visiting their favorite saloon in the area, ranging from Calamity Jane to Wild Bill Hickok, who at one time called Hays, a nearby town, their home.

Wyatt Earp, with the reputation of being serious and loyal, no doubt ventured through Rome on his way from Wichita to Dodge. Earp, spare with his words and not eager to fire off his pistol, learned months later that the combination of a cholera outbreak and the decision to bring the railroad to

Hays led to the demise of Rome. Just over 150 years later, I met the new sheriff in Hays, Wyatt Fullmer, who approaches his brewmaster responsibilities with a steady hand and serious mindset.

Just as Earp and Fullmer share a first name, the latter, brewmaster at Lb. Brewing Company in Hays, had the same serious approach to our book visit. Wyatt was spare with his comments while he and his assistant brewer Ryan Engel worked in their brewhouse.

Kevin, my in-law, and I sat down in Gella's amid the energy and great brewery noise, at a table that suddenly

Kevin Lorenz, my in-law and good friend, happily stunned with ten-plus tasters at Gella's Diner & Lb. Brewing, Hays, Kansas. *Author's collection.*

was covered with fourteen tasters for each of us. We have great memories of the award-winning beer covering our table. We had a blast tasting the array of styles of "liquid bread" (origins of the brewery name "Lb."). The energy from the many loyal customers was contagious in this successful venture, spearheaded twenty years ago by a group of investors. Gella's became a cornerstone in the Hays downtown revitalization.

Wyatt is the third brewmaster at Lb. since it opened. The first brewmaster, Gerald Evans, is a legend. He has since retired to Brownell and his farm but had an amazing impact on the Kansas craft brewing industry, training aspiring assistant brewers who are now head brewers at spots like Defiance Brewing and Wichita Brewing Company. He also trained the second brewmaster at Lb., Brendan Arnold, who has moved on to become head brewer at Alternate Ending Beer Company in Aberdeen, New Jersey. Arnold played an influential role in mentoring Wyatt, when Fullmer served as his assistant. Wyatt, who never homebrewed, earned the opportunity to move into the brewhouse at Gella's as assistant brewer. He stepped up into the brewmaster position two years ago and has continued delivering great brews made from simple ingredients, grounded with respect for the traditions of German brewing. Wyatt told me that the pressure he embraces is to ensure that the team is keeping up with the beer production to satisfy the thirst of the locals and I-70 road trippers.

Ryan took a moment to say, "Wyatt is a sponge, dude,"[19] skilled in retention of the processes and one hundred plus recipes at Lb. The longer I spent with Wyatt, interviewing him as he worked in the brewhouse, the more

I appreciated his stoic style and understood why Lb. Brewing continues to deliver great beer.

Wyatt is the third generation of brewmasters at Lb. and is on point stylistically with the broad selection of beer on tap. Ryan, assistant brewer (and beekeeper on the side), captured the magic at Lb.: "The sociality of beer is cool because you meet new people and see regulars five days a week."[20] He paused and nailed why we all enjoy hanging out at breweries and why my first book trip with Kevin was so memorable, saying, "There is something deeply human about drinking beer."[21]

8. CENTER PIVOT RESTAURANT & BREWERY

300 Main Street * Quinter, Kansas 67752
785-754-2332
www.centerpivotbrewery.com
www.facebook.com/Center-Pivot-Restaurant-and-Brewery
Brewing System: 1BBL

Center Pivot Brewery stands alone among all the breweries across our Sunshine State. This one-barrel brewery led by Steve Nicholson (owner and head brewer) brews some of the most unique and drinkable beer that I have enjoyed as I have written this book. Steve is a gentle giant, standing at six feet, nine inches tall—easy to spot whether at a beer festival or in his

#CNTRPVT, Center Pivot in Quinter, watched over by Steve's faithful three: Milo, BB and Maizee. *Author's collection.*

141

brewery. He also has three loyal partners in his faithful labs Milo, BB and Maizee, who proudly complement the license plate while hanging out on the tailgate. Steve's brewing approach starts with a focus on tradition, adding creativity and a boldness that shows itself across his beer selection.

How did Steve arrive here? To create what he has in this rural Kansas town of 911 people was a tall task. He and his wife, Ericka, moved to Quinter knowing that Steve would step in as a teacher and coach at their high school. The couple had what could have been an insurmountable obstacle had it not been for their persistence, commitment and personable approach. Quinter shifted from a dry Kansas community to one that now supports Center Pivot. The single-barrel system came from the Copper Kettle in Aurora, Colorado. That restaurant and brewery had outgrown the equipment, which was exactly what Steve was looking for.

Expect five Center Pivot beers on draft complemented by a guest beer tap grouping that brings any style that might be your preference to the table. The creativity in his brewing has led to first-time experiences for me, starting with his Cracked Pepper Cream Ale and continuing to the Spruce Is Loose winter beer. Inspiration for any brewer can come from multiple directions. In these cases, a taste of an ale with pepper at the Great American Beer Festival started his hunt for the right balance, while the Spruce Is Loose beer originated in Norway and Scandinavia, later becoming a colonial recipe.

Nothing makes Steve feel better than when a customer asks for a second pint. He told me and my in-law, Kevin, "It's not work."[22] It is worth the trip to Quinter to be part of the local community that gathers at CPR&B, to have a meal and know that whatever Center Pivot style you choose will be enjoyed.

Chapter 9

GOING PRO

Have you ever thought of opening your own brewery? Are you an avid homebrewer with a following of family and friends? After receiving great feedback on a typical Saturday brew day at home, surrounded by your fans, have you caught yourself thinking about taking your brewing to the next step?

I have a hunch that at least one of these questions resonates with you. Why wouldn't it?! Brewing beer, for many, began with a starter kit and expanded through time into a more robust setup as the passion project became an obsession. About 96 percent of the professional brewers across Kansas started as homebrewers.

All the brewers across our state have their own unique stories about how they evolved from homebrewing to making a living creating and serving great craft beer. My hope is that the brewer stories and the insights offered might make you pause and contemplate becoming part of the craft beer industry.

The first story starts in Independence, Kansas, at Indy Brew Works. Tim Hardy, head brewer, watched his dad homebrew in their garage. This progressed to both men attending Siebel Institute. Ultimately, Tim landed a professional brewing position in time to help open the Brew Works doors for the first time.

Tim and his mom became "assistant brewers" in the family operation, improving process efficiencies. The Hardy household garage brewhouse grew, resulting in Tim and his dad working side by side on their own systems.

The tipping point for Tim was a trip that the three took to Colorado. The days were mapped out with brewery visits. Aspiring brewers have been inspired by visits to Denver and Fort Collins brewery scenes. The two decided to go to the Siebel Institute in Chicago, which is one of the top brewing schools in the United States.

The training and certification process with Siebel was amazing. They were the first father-and-son pair to graduate together with certifications. The classwork included long stints in Chicago, as well as across the pond in Munich. Siebel was invaluable in lighting a fire in Tim to become a head brewer. I had the opportunity to check out his school textbooks, his class material and schedules and was impressed with the structure and the balance of process and art in which he and his dad were immersed.

Thanks to Robert and Jessica Box, owners of Indy Brew Works, Tim was given a brewhouse blank canvas. Tim approached going pro methodically, brewing true to the style heritage, offering a good range of styles for the Brew Works community. I have visited the team frequently in pursuit of capturing this story about Tim's journey. He is a talented brewer, grounded in process, stepping out and showing his creativity with twists on classic styling.

For our second story, meet master brewer Larry Cook, who owns Dodge City Brewing. Larry started homebrewing in 2005. He shared with me that he brewed what he loved at the time, leaning into IPAs, confessing that he was a hophead back in the day. What started as a serious hobby for Larry became a compulsion as his knowledge of the brewing process and pursuit of making a better beer drove him. Larry had a career as a certified public accountant, which required significant travel. As he traveled, a business acquaintance and friend joined him frequently in an after-hours pursuit of visiting breweries.

Larry eventually came to a fork in the road of life and opted to make the right turn toward taking his obsession for making great beer to the highest level. Dodge City Brewing opened twelve years after his craft beer pilgrimage started. Larry is so driven to brew the best beer for his customers that a recipe could be tinkered with more than forty times.

One of the best things that I have learned about Larry is that while focused on elevating the craft, he also pursued certification through the Beer Judge Certification Program. He does not hesitate to share his knowledge with other brewers, providing feedback on new brews or offering tips on process and brewing equipment. While I was at a homebrew competition in November, hosted by the Walnut River Brewing team, I had a conversation with a young brewer who clearly had a passion and a dream that he was chasing. His homebrew equipment was used, sold to him by Larry Cook. The future for beer fans in Kansas is bright because of great brewers inspiring the next generation.

These two individuals have had unique journeys in the industry. Tim is an example of a homebrewer taking the school certification route. He now is head brewer and is evolving his skills, getting more creative and focusing in on what his community wants. Think about Larry Cook and his obsession for making the 1872 pilsner perfect. His work is evidence of how intent he is on delivering great beer to the community. His passion spreads across the state as he coaches homebrewers and professional brewers alike.

The next chapter, "Santa Fe Trail," includes just three breweries. Travel the miles from Dodge to Garden City along the Mountain Route of the Trail, with the opportunity to visit Flat Mountain and Hidden Trail, a newbie in 2021. The miles are hundreds and the breweries few, but the pint waiting for you is worth it.

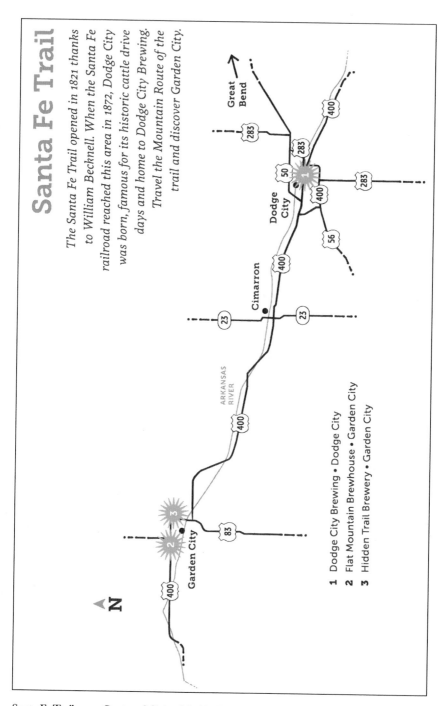

Santa Fe Trail

The Santa Fe Trail opened in 1821 thanks to William Becknell. When the Santa Fe railroad reached this area in 1872, Dodge City was born, famous for its historic cattle drive days and home to Dodge City Brewing. Travel the Mountain Route of the trail and discover Garden City.

N

Great Bend →

283

400

283

283

50

400

Dodge City

56

400

Cimarron

23

23

ARKANSAS RIVER

400

400

83

Garden City

400

1 Dodge City Brewing • Dodge City
2 Flat Mountain Brewhouse • Garden City
3 Hidden Trail Brewery • Garden City

Santa Fe Trail map. *Courtesy of Christy Schneider, Inkello Design & Letterpress, East Lawrence, Kansas.*

Chapter 10

SANTA FE TRAIL

1. DODGE CITY BREWING

701 3rd Avenue * Dodge City, Kansas 67801
620-371-3999
www.dodgecitybrewing.com
www.facebook.com/dodgecitybrewing
Brewing System: 5BBL

"I love talking about beer,"[1] Larry Cook, owner and master brewer, said with a contagious energy as we sat on his patio on a beautiful early evening at Dodge City Brewing. We found our way to the brewery after an enlightening tour of the Boot Hill Museum. What we witnessed during our time at Dodge City was a life and energy created by his customers who were enjoying great pizza and a nice lineup of beer styles.

As I reflect on my time with Larry, a BJCP-certified beer judge and longtime homebrewer, the headline was his obsession for his brewery and beer. This is best highlighted by the conversation we had about his 1872 Lager, a pre-Prohibition style that our great-granddads might have enjoyed. Larry surprised me at first when he said, "I still can't stop. This 1872 I have done forty batches of. I just keep looking for something to make it better."[2]

Larry realized his dreams with the opening of DCB in July 2017. He walked away from years of being a CPA, wanting to pursue his passion:

The author on the Dodge City Brewing patio, with twelve tasters. *Courtesy of Kevin Lorenz.*

brewing quality craft beer. He had a client in Wichita that inspired this drive to take his award-winning years of homebrewing to the professional level. The two traveled for fifteen years, visiting dozens of breweries not only to enjoy a pint but also to check out the production side of the breweries. "I have a passion for good beer,"[3] Larry definitively stated.

Expect to find up to eleven beer styles on tap that will satisfy any beer fan. As you taste your first pint, know that Larry has worked to exhaustion on a weekly basis, pushing his passion for the craft to new levels. Larry confessed that he had been a hophead back in his early brewing years. "I am now post-IPA and in my lager phase,"[4] he said.

Travel to Dodge knowing that you can count on great pizza and an array of beer styles that will satisfy any taste. Larry brings his talents to the brewhouse each and every day with the intent to make a beer he is proud of that will quench your thirst. Take the time to talk with Larry about his beer, knowing that he will be happy to dive into flavors and expectations, like during my experience when he said that the beer had a "nice caramel character, with leather on the back end of it."[5]

#Strivingforperfection

2. FLAT MOUNTAIN BREWHOUSE

207 North Main Street * Garden City, Kansas 67846
620-260-2886
flatmountainbrewhouse.com
www.facebook.com/FlatMountainBrewhouse
Brewing System: 7BBL

Flat Mountain Brewhouse is the first of two breweries to grace the Garden City landscape. It opened in 2019, becoming a destination for a quality

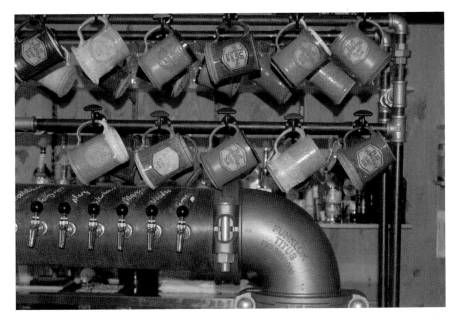

At the bar at Flat Mountain Brewhouse in Garden City, Kansas. Kevin and I checked out the tap setup. *Author's collection.*

food menu and twelve rotating taps. Three families united with the goal of opening FMB on Main Street as part of its downtown revitalization, creating a welcoming environment for everyone.

The three couples had two things in common going into this project. They all liked to drink beer and collectively knew little about opening a professional brewhouse. With the help of a Garden City Community College professor who had a decade of homebrewing experience, the brewhouse team started brewing.

Flat Mountain Brewhouse was on my first travel on the seven-month-long road trip. I had the opportunity to meet Rob Gardner, new in his brewing position at the brewhouse. Initially brought in by the management team to run the front of the house, Rob was later promoted to general manager. When the two former brewers left, the brewhouse needed someone to step in. Rob, a novice at brewing, took the leap.

Rob impressed me with his level of enthusiasm and self-awareness that he had so much to learn. The good news at the time was that only four of the twelve rotating taps were brewhouse taps. That setup alleviated early pressure on Rob, as he worked hard to learn the system and master brewing the core beers with consistency. My in-law, Kevin, who was on this western

Kansas road trip with me, walked away from the visit in agreement with me that Rob was on the right track.

As I write this, seven months later, the Brewhouse website has six beers listed on tap that are Flat Mountain styles. Flat Mountain is primarily a restaurant, with the brewhouse taking a backseat in priority. The challenge for Rob in 2022 is a big one. He has the core beers taken care of. Stepping up the experimental and trendy styles will give the folks in Garden City two good brewery options to enjoy.

3. HIDDEN TRAIL BREWING

2010 East Schulman Avenue * Garden City, Kansas 67846
620-315-4690
www.hiddentrailbrewing.com
www.facebook.com/HiddenTrailBrewing
Brewing System: 5BBL

"It is going to be exciting,"[6] Jude Cundiff, son of co-owner and brewer Cody, shared with me as I prepared to leave the team at Hidden Trail. The day I visited, Michael Cole, co-owner and brewer, greeted me at the construction site with Kansas winds blowing one-hundred-degree Garden City air through the building. Michael walked me through the brewhouse space, sharing their plans, as the heat hit us hard.

The team's focus is on creating a family-friendly environment in the restored barn next to the Talley Trail. While parents enjoy a pint of their favorite Hidden Trail pour, little and big kids can play Pac-Man, pinball and foosball. The space encourages patrons to become family with strangers, sharing a communal table. The barn itself stands alone among the brewery buildings across our state. Built in the 1940s, the structure was originally a granary, which makes it fitting to see a brewery take over the space. When I visited the construction site, Michael shared their vision as we dodged contractors. I believed in what he was saying despite the dust, the noise and the shell of a barn. Craft beer fans will not be disappointed when making the trek.

Cody, co-owner and dad to Jude, passionately shared how he approaches the general education psychology classes he teaches at Garden City Community College, which is just down the street from Hidden Trail. He is

Grab a pint at Hidden Trail Brewing, located on the Talley Trail. *Courtesy of Hidden Trail Brewing, Garden City, Kansas.*

pouring his passion into teaching and opening the eyes of his students to the pressing issues of mental illness. Building awareness and creating the ability to be empathetic to those struggling are two of Cody's goals. His drive to make the world a better place carries over to a strong set of beliefs shared by the three that are present today through activities like the patio garden plantings open to the community to create.

I asked the team what they want their patrons to remember after visiting Hidden Trail. Michael responded, saying, "We are a group of humble guys, chasing our dream. I want people to enjoy hanging out here. I want Hidden Trail to be a big Garden City thing. I want people to see Hidden Trail and its association with Garden."[7]

Expect to see the trio at the brewery whenever you visit. Cody and Michael had twenty-plus years of combined homebrewing experiences under their belts before they went pro, brewing at Flat Mountain Restaurant across town in Garden City. They passionately talk about the styles, their taste profiles and the beer names. As the brewery settles into a rhythm since opening in late November 2021, the team plans to give back to the community. They are tossing ideas around that will affect the youth in the city, ranging from establishing a scholarship program to helping fund new football uniforms for local teams. Cody brought it all home to me as we stood at the front of the brewery. Two of his children, Jude and Demetria, were nearby as he said, "You are never going to change the world. The opportunity is to change your little world. I want to make people proud to be here, to hang out here."[8]

Chapter 11

IT'S A SMALL TOWN STICKING AROUND

Yeah, kicking it old school, it's a small town sticking around
Just like folks used to, good ol' boys and girls
Just falling in love, living the life, yeah
Middle of nowhere feels about right
Keep it old school, just the way we like
Old school
—*Toby Keith, lyrics from "Peso in My Pocket"*[1]

Mike McVey, co-owner and brewer at Transport Brewery, asked me what the most significant story was that I had captured visiting the breweries across our state, gathering wonderful content for this book. I did not pause for long before sharing with Mike what I was thankful to have experienced.

My answer came to life as I recorded my thoughts while driving north on state highway 183. Toby Keith, whose song came on at the same time in the background, spoke to me at the right time, the right place and for the right reason.

The words in this story came easily, fueled by my racing mind, thinking about the possibilities for our state. Miles of Kansas highways, ripe with panoramic views that have been enchanting, have given me strength of thought during the solitude. I have been taken aback as I have driven through those rural Kansas communities, which are dying like that last grape on a vine. I have looked out at what used to be vibrant main streets, now nothing but streets of shuttered buildings.

What has been so inspiring on this trip has been seeing other rural Kansas towns such as Council Grove, Courtland, Holton, Humboldt, Minneapolis and Phillipsburg, each with populations of under 2,500 citizens. The main thoroughfares in these towns buzz with activity now, fueled by new destinations such as the breweries; they are anything but ghost towns.

These brewery owners are "kicking it old school," with a new twist. Their perspective is a balance of old soul and new thinking that is community minded. They have taken that leap while making their dream a reality. I have been humbled as I grasp the shared commitment and belief in this group that they want to have influence in their communities.

I am seeing a youth movement as well. I am meeting people my daughters' ages, maintaining their full-time jobs while putting their sweat equity into bringing buildings dating from the turn of the century back to life. What is so admirable is the mindset that I have captured through long conversations built on the belief that they can make a difference. Not necessarily by changing the world, but cognizant that they can improve their communities. I see a story that needs to be told. I see a story that is heartwarming and exciting for our Sunflower State.

In the past, Kansas towns were centered on a thriving farming industry or a single major employer. Times changed, jobs were eliminated, young people migrated out of town and life went on. All the while, the backbone in these towns stayed resolute and the community pride held firm. New generations of town officials knew that they had to think differently than their parents. Suddenly, each of these communities is turning a page in the book of life to a new chapter.

What do these six towns with new breweries have in common? They are intertwined. As my thoughts took shape, I visualized a ball of twine in front of me. Each piece of twine is held by a person who either grew up in one of these communities or was seeking a simpler life. The ball of twine started to take shape as I thought about the shared motivations that brought these owners home, including moving closer to family, creating a richer life for one's family and wanting to make a difference in a rural Kansas town.

Most of these brewery owners encountered city committees that knew the importance of not saying no. Marci Penner, executive director and founder of the nonprofit Kansas Sampler Foundation,[2] captured what these towns are doing to open the doors to entrepreneurship and downtown revitalization. She said, "To me, what is so important is to let young people do their thing, to encourage them. We just have to create this environment that they want to be part of. The kids will start coming back."[3]

Council Grove could be the model for successful rural Kansas town revitalization. Recovery and growth cannot happen unless there are committed and visionary people affiliated with the town development council, the town leadership, the county's development organization, nonprofits such as Kansas Sampler Foundation and brewery owners like the team at Riverbank Brewing—all ready to engage and find ways to say yes.

Tracy Henry, executive director of the Greater Morris County Development Corporation, captured the vibe needed, which has been unleashed in charming Council Grove, saying that "activity creates activity."[4] In her role, as with her peers across our state, she is that resource and supporting actor who realizes that her job "isn't to tell somebody that it is going to work or that it isn't going to work. My job is to say, tell me how it is going to work and what I can do to help you make it work."[5]

Downtown Council Grove has gone through a metamorphosis over the last six years, taking down shutters on more than a dozen storefronts with new businesses coming to town, including Flint Hills Books, Watts Coffee Company, The Wooden Spoon, Flowers by Lindsey, Alexander ArtWorks, Adams Lumber & Homestore and Cami's Cake Company. Jennifer M. Kassebaum, owner of Flint Hills Books, captured the spirit of these owners, saying, "Adams Lumber is also an example of a family-owned business where the next generation has stayed in Council Grove to work in this community. I applaud the work and dedication of each of these young business owners to their hometown."[6]

Tracy was instrumental in getting the state to recognize Council Grove as an E-Community, selected by the nonprofit NetWork Kansas as an entrepreneurship community.[7] The nonprofit group supports projects for just under sixty-six communities across the state, giving them access to capital. For entrepreneurs, the short-term loans and fixed interest rates can be beneficial, serving as that gap financing needed to make a dream become real.

Meet Jesse Knight, co-owner with his wife, Deidre, and three other partners of Riverbank Brewing. Jesse, who grew up on a farm outside of Altavista, went to high school in Council Grove. While there, he forged a friendship with Joshua Gant, who along with his wife, Lindsay, have become co-owners as well of Riverbank. These four epitomize what Toby Keith's lyrics speak to:

> *Middle of nowhere feels about right / Keep it old school, just the way we like / Old school.*[8]

I first sat with Jesse, Deidre and Lindsay in the midsummer of 2021. The beliefs they shared have stuck with me since that afternoon. Jesse talked about Council Grove and coming home, saying, "Maybe our age group is starting to understand that this way of life is attractive."[9] Lindsay mentioned, "The connection started with the four of us. We started dreaming bigger."[10]

Jesse, who has served on the Greater Morris County Development board with Deidre, has also sat on the Council Grove City Council. Their commitment to the community is strong. They know that if Riverbank Brewing is successful, it will be because they have created a "place for people to gather, to kind of share that community aspect."[11]

They started dreaming about creating something that would give people a reason to come to their Kansas town. Jesse underscored the value that the two couples, in addition to the fifth partner, Pat Atchity, are bringing to Council Grove. "We want people to know what it feels like to live here, to visit here."[12]

Celebrating Marci Penner and all she does in leading the Kansas Sampler Foundation that she and her father, Milferd Penner, founded in 1993 is a fitting to end this story about the success and vibrancy in our state and rural communities.

Remember that ball of twine? On my book journey, two people I met held twines that connected back to Marci and her inspiring work. Luke Mahin is co-owner with his wife, Jennifer, of another rural town brewery success story, Irrigation Ales in his hometown of Courtland. He thanks Marci for helping him network across the state with like-minded entrepreneurs. Luke introduced me to a study that Marci and her team at Kansas Sampler Foundation authored, called "Kansas Power Up & Go: The Action Report."[13] The second individual, Tracy Henry, succinctly captured how she feels about the impact Marci has had on the state, telling me, "Marci Penner, she is the bomb."[14]

The mission for the Kansas Sampler Foundation is "to preserve and sustain rural culture by educating Kansans about Kansas and networking and supporting rural communities."[15] I drove out to Inman to meet with

Marci at her foundation. I understood how impactful this soft-spoken woman with a huge heart and drive to elevate our state and rural communities has been. As Marci said so eloquently, "I just follow my nose."[16] I learned more about the role she plays in our state with people like the Knights in Council Grove and the Mahins in Courtland. Kansas Sampler Foundation works to facilitate grass-roots conversations and actions while bringing the committed voices together.

A goal of the Kansas Sampler Foundation is "to keep every town viable that shows the will and spirit to help itself." Marci utilizes the space in Inman as a place to gather key voices from across the state to have dialogue, forge connections and be in the fight with others who are ambassadors of change.

Marci is not one to yearn for the spotlight. In fact, she spent more time learning about my book, which truly does celebrate the communities and people across this state that are doing their part to strengthen the sense of belonging. She became my cheerleader, as she does with any new connection she makes in our Sunflower State. Marci started brainstorming about inviting microbrewery owners to Inman along with people who want to understand how community happens. She said, "Your book could be a conduit to bringing people together. The lieutenant governor would come to a roundtable discussion so electric as how microbreweries in Kansas have helped shape these communities."[17]

Marci is a champion of our state, a cheerleader for young Kansans who want to become business owners. She is purpose-driven, looking for opportunities to create coalitions and connect entrepreneurs with their peers from around the state. Marci also is focused on building the infrastructure for greater communication and action to support the efforts to make rural life more viable. A key finding in the report, done in collaboration with the Office of Prosperity, is that by creating a place that everyone is proud to call home, we will be affecting the state's future through these vibrant communities.[18]

That sense of pride for community can be seen in the three towns—Pittsburg, Independence and Humboldt—that are home to the four breweries in the next chapter. Enjoy "Coal Fields to Little House on the Prairie" by adding a stop at the Laura Ingalls Wilder home while visiting Indy Brew Works in Independence or the Miners Hall Museum in Franklin.

Remember what Toby Keith's lyrics spoke to at the outset of this story? While driving north on state Highway 183, the lyrics impacted me viscerally. Those words, "Just falling in love, living the life, yeah, middle of nowhere feels about right,"[19] are exactly what Marci has captured in her study: "I am ecstatic about their passion and commitment for living rural by choice."[20]

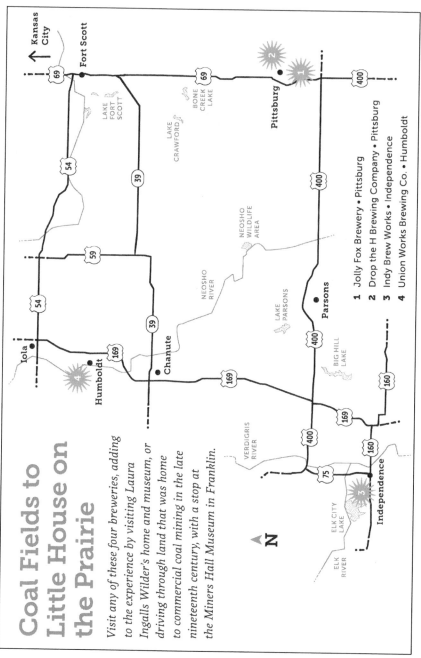

Coal Fields to Little House on the Prairie

Visit any of these four breweries, adding to the experience by visiting Laura Ingalls Wilder's home and museum, or driving through land that was home to commercial coal mining in the late nineteenth century, with a stop at the Miners Hall Museum in Franklin.

1 Jolly Fox Brewery • Pittsburg
2 Drop the H Brewing Company • Pittsburg
3 Indy Brew Works • Independence
4 Union Works Brewing Co. • Humboldt

Coal Fields to Little House on the Prairie map. *Courtesy of Christy Schneider, Inkello Design & Letterpress, East Lawrence, Kansas.*

Chapter 12

COAL FIELDS TO LITTLE HOUSE ON THE PRAIRIE

1. THE JOLLY FOX BREWERY

301 South Broadway * Pittsburg, Kansas 66762
620-670-5999
www.jollyfoxbrew.com
www.facebook.com/jollyfoxbrew
Brewing System: 10BBL

"I make great beer,"[1] Joel Stewart, owner and head brewer at Jolly Fox, said to me in our first minutes together. This came from a guy who at one point helped open a Missouri winery and was honored with a silver medal for one of his wines. What is his secret sauce? Joel started working in the industry at twenty, building a deep understanding of winemaking, the fermenting process and brewing.

When deciding what to brew at Jolly Fox, he is straightforward with his approach: "My philosophy on beer making is to keep it simple and make it great. There is no need to complicate the grain bill. You focus on yeast, grain and hops and see how you can marry those in a simplistic form that makes a great beer."[2]

When Joel came back to Pittsburg, he started formulating an idea for his business with the goal of becoming self-employed. His strongest marketable skill was his brewing talent, which had been fine-tuned over a decade of

Two beer flights at Jolly Fox Brewery in Pittsburg, Kansas. Foxxy IPA caught my attention. *Author's collection.*

homebrewing. He has a friend who frequently hammered him over the head with the idea that Joel should go pro.

Joel, inspired by a sighting of a fox near their home's front porch, came up with the name Jolly Fox. You will have a fun time and tasty craft beer to your liking when visiting. Joel does an excellent job of marketing his business and offering weekly events, from trivia nights to Whiskey Wednesdays, which have created a loyal following. He looked at me at one point and said, "I can't fuck this up....I have people coming from over two hours away to enjoy my beer and brewery."[3]

Relationships are important to Joel. Jolly Fox is intertwined with the community through collaborations with local coffeehouses and support of other small businesses (such as Books & Burrow) and through a whiskey club that gathers throughout the year back in the brewhouse for specific whiskey tastings. I was invited to talk about my book at the opening of a scotch whiskey tasting in early December. Joel shared thoughts about the flavor profiles and history behind each distillery as a dozen of us had the opportunity to have our taste buds challenged as well as our knowledge of scotch whiskeys strengthened.

In the future, Joel hopes to expand his business to include a distillery. He has the knowledge and passion in the world of whiskeys to make it possible. Supporting Jolly Fox is easy. They live locally, work locally (his wife is an assistant superintendent in the school system), collaborate locally and consistently deliver quality craft beer to his fans in Pittsburg and surrounding communities. Do yourself a favor and follow them on Facebook. There is no doubt that Joel will offer an event or a fresh style that will draw you to the Fox.

2. DROP THE H BREWING COMPANY

107 East Rose Street * Pittsburg, Kansas 66762
620-404-4019
droptheh.com
www.facebook.com/DropTheHBrewingCompany
Brewing System: 7BBL

"Let's Talk Beer" is a series of entertaining, informative and short videos that Mark McClain plays supporting actor in, with the feature beer the star of the show. You can find these on the brewery Facebook page. Long term, Mark plans to have a link embedded in each beer style listed on the Drop the H website, which will be one-of-a-kind in Kansas. Not only will you be able to check out what is on tap on the way to Pittsburg, but you will be able to take it a step further, getting pulled into the story and, if nothing else, increasing your thirst for that first pint!

As Mark and I settled in for a great visit, he shared with me that he and his wife, Cathy, had a mission statement for Drop the H that underscored the word *craft*. Customers walking through the doors the first time at 107 East Rose Street can expect "craft beer, craft pizza, craft experience." I want to bring you back to the early 1920s to share what craft product was once on display and for sale in this gorgeous building.

William "Billy" Durant, once CEO of General Motors, established Durant Motors Inc. after being terminated by GM.[4] Billy developed a line of cars designed to compete with Buick price points, while also designing luxury cars to compete against Cadillac. One hundred years ago, the brewery space held American crafted cars that might have dazzled the Pittsburg community, but in time, they did not gain the popularity needed to avoid the end of Durant Motors.

The next time you visit, sit in a booth under the brick arched windows, glance toward the beautiful brewhouse and think about the folks who might

Drop the H Brewing Company flights. *Courtesy of Drop the H Brewing Company, Pittsburg, Kansas.*

have been standing in your spot a century ago, kicking a tire. Pause a moment as well to understand that the owners are both retired U.S. Air Force KC-135 pilots. Their life together also pulls them apart. Mark serves as a pilot and trainer for Delta Airlines. Cathy serves as chair of the Board of Directors at the Air Force Academy in addition to her CEO responsibilities for Dauntless Leadership, LLC, which she founded. After I thanked Mark for his military service, he humbly responded, "It was my honor and privilege to serve."[5] If you have the opportunity, make sure to thank them both for their service.

Mark fell in love with craft beer while his family lived in Germany. He went to high school there and enjoyed the biergartens that he and his friends frequented, learning to appreciate great beer at a youthful age.

He believes that brewpubs should be integral parts of the life in their communities. Mark and Cathy have created a "community tank," through which they pick a local charity and have members from it help in the brewing process, resulting in that beer going from the serving tank directly to a tap. All proceeds from that tap go directly to that charity, which thus far has affected Big Brothers Big Sisters Crawford County and VetLinks.org. Their military service instills the focus on the mission, which in the case of VetLinks.org is a commitment to our veterans and their families affected by post-traumatic stress disorder.

Mark approaches his brewing at Drop the H true to the style profiles. One will find around seven styles on tap, with a wide variety of taste profiles ranging from the LCL "LOCAL" lager to the Rose Street red ale. Mark tries to get as close as he can to the German beer purity law, known as *reinheitsgebot*,[6] which went into law in 1516, dictating that the only ingredients Germans could brew with were malt, hops and water. He quipped, "I might not technically be a *reinheitsgebot* brewer but am pretty darn close! *Prost.*"[7]

3. INDY BREW WORKS

223 West Main Street * Independence, Kansas 67301
620-577-2162
www.indybrewworks.com
www.facebook.com/indybrewworks
Brewing System: 5BBL

It is hard not to imagine seeing seventeen-year-old Mickey Mantle walk out the tunnel at Shulthis Stadium on East Oak Street in Independence, Kansas, get into his car and head down to Indy Brew Works to celebrate. His first professional home run as a minor-league player for the Independence Yankees cleared the center field fence and traveled close to 460 feet.

Today, home plate stands 5,280 feet from Indy Brew Works, the local watering hole for a good craft beer. I bet Mickey would have sat down with Tim Hardy, the head brewer, and had a pint or two or three of the Irish Red if their lives intersected.

Mickey, who struggled at first for the Independence Yankees and called his dad to say he was quitting, could relate to the struggles Robert and Jessica Box had over three years of trying to open a brewery. After being insulted by a banker who would not even look at the two-hundred-plus-page business plan, Robert told Jessica that he was 100 percent done with trying to make this happen.

Good things happen to those who do not give up. Mickey fought his way through his slump as shortstop for the Yankees and went on to have a Hall of Fame career. A week after Robert waved the white flag, he had the opportunity to choose the building downtown that would be the brewery's home, saving their historic structure from imminent demolition.

Indy Brew Works had its second anniversary in November 2021. The team had incredible support from the community, starting with the bank president, who looked at Robert and said, "We want you here." Robert, who

Top: Tim Hardy, head brewer, and Robert Box, owner, loving the brewery life at Indy Brew Works in Independence, Kansas. *Author's collection.*

Bottom: A local businessperson and retired firefighter gifted this flag to Indy Brew Works and Robert Box (Coffeyville firefighter), honoring all firefighters. *Author's collection.*

is also a firefighter in Coffeyville, was appreciative of the town's support. One loyal customer, a local businessperson and former firefighter himself, crafted an American flag in metal with flames at the tips of the stripes to honor all firefighters and gifted it to the brewery. Robert and Jessica look back fondly at their time in Raleigh, North Carolina, where they fell in love with craft beer, happy that they pushed through the difficulties of opening a small business.

The two forged a friendship with Tim Hardy while living in Lubbock, Texas. Tim came from a homebrewing family, joining his dad to earn Siebel Institute certification in master brewing and as a brewmaster. He told me that the greatest impact he felt from his U.S. and German training was his deep appreciation and knowledge about the brewing process and the beauty and uniqueness of ingredients that translate into good beer.

Indy Brew Works has a tap list that will satisfy anyone's thirst. Tim stays true stylistically, offering a bevy of great ales starting with the Irish Red. He has converted beer fans in Busch Light country to his drinkable and balanced selection. Expect traditional German styling and techniques in Tim's brewhouse. He has an enthusiastic group of fans, including downtown lawyers, who make a habit of visiting for a pint any time he introduces a small-batch test or experimental beer.

4. UNION WORKS BREWING COMPANY

919 North 8th Street * Humboldt, Kansas 66748
www.facebook.com/unionworksco
Brewing System: 10BBL

Union Works Brewing Company is a blend of two amazing stories. The first celebrates a Humboldt family who goes back five generations. For the Works family, the risks they took in 1857 as they plowed forward on their farmland near Humboldt were as daunting as the risks the newer generation made investing in their town, 150 years later. The second story focuses on a University of Kansas graduate who left home and the United States for a life afar that culminated with him taking a huge risk in wine country in Bosnia, opening a brewery in a country that did not appreciate craft beer at the time.

The small, rural Kansas community of Humboldt has a celebrated history.[8] Humboldt is famous for being the home of Walter "Big Train" Johnson, who was one of the five inaugural members inducted into the Cooperstown Baseball Hall of Fame. Humboldt is infamous for suffering through two Confederate raids, including one in late 1861 when most of the town was burned down. Seven years later, the Humboldt Brewery opened on the banks of the Neosho River. H.C. Brendecke, owner and brewer, was ready to help and donate for the "upbuilding" of the city. Tony Works, developer of Union Works Brewing Company and one of four of his dad Joe's children, has combined talent and effort with his siblings to create the organization A Bolder Humboldt, focused on developing a strong future.

Brendecke and Works, the two separated by more than a century, aspired to create community through local beer, while spending time and money for the greater good of Humboldt. When I wrapped up my first conversation with Tony, we stepped outside to look at downtown. Tony was discussing what needed to happen in Humboldt to be able to recruit talented young people such as a chef for his brewery, and he added, "That's what really is our mantra for what we are doing. Our touchstone is always, 'Let's make this a place where we want to live.' It may keep this town from dying."[9]

Tony and his team started renovation of a former Wonder Bread building, just outside of downtown. They are building a brewery that will offer an array of beer styles, while also offering elevated dining with casual family space and quieter space for a more intimate experience. When the brewery opens, their spacious patio beer garden will be one of the largest among all Kansas breweries. Tony and his siblings started dreaming of opening a brewery back in 2015. Year after year, they would dream of having a pint on the patio. Jump forward to 2022, when they will enjoy that pint, brewed by the new head brewer at Union Works.

Works described the discovery of his brewer, Andrew Monfort, saying that the story "is about leaving home, doing cool things and coming back."[10] When Monfort decided that working in refineries as a chemical engineer was not what he wanted to do long term, he headed overseas, taught and then cycled through Asia and Europe before settling down in Trebinje, Bosnia. Andrew opened his small brewery, OZ Craft Pivo, as a pioneer at that time, in a country that had not witnessed craft beer growth. The blood, sweat and tears he poured into the business were no different than what any other brewery owner has experienced in Kansas. What was different were the smuggling trips he had to take, hiding beer ingredients, equipment and tools in his luggage as he came back into Bosnia.

When COVID shut down Europe for months, Andrew explored nascent ideas about moving his business home. When he learned that there was a budding brewery in Allen County, he reached out to Works. The connection seemed fortuitous for both.

Tony, who has more than a decade of homebrewing under his belt, likes all beer varieties and has an experimental spirit within him. Andrew is focused on filling the ten taps at Union Works with styles that the town and those traveling into Humboldt want. Expect a lager to be a flagship style, complemented by a lineup that even the "Big Train" would be intimidated by, ranging from IPAs to seasonal selections.

Tony reminisced with me, saying, "The industry is kind of coming full circle...where you brew locally and drink what's brewed locally."[11] Union Works Brewing Company in Humboldt, with a population of just under 1,800 people, is one of the rural town success stories across the state where breweries are opening. Works concluded by saying, "We'll find what people want. I like thinking about that period where every town had their own little brewery. I think that's where things have wanted to go for a long time."[12]

AFTERWORD

What is next for our Sunflower State? The good news for Kansas craft beer fans is that our craft brewery growth is outpacing the national average as of 2020. The number of Kansas breweries at the end of 2020 increased by just under 7 percent.[1] Nationally, growth in the industry increased 4.5 percent.[2] Regionally, our rate of growth has exceeded several of our neighboring states, including Colorado, Iowa and Nebraska. The anomaly is Oklahoma, which has seen an explosion in growth since a key liquor law was changed. Craft beer fans in the state just south of us have 22 percent more breweries to visit than they did just one year ago.[3]

As I look toward late spring 2022, I know of four new breweries working hard to open their doors. Friction Beer Company in Shawnee, Transport Brewery (second location) in Gardner, Baldwin City Beer Company in Baldwin and Stockyards Brewing Company in Overland Park (second location but first in Kansas) will be bringing new experiences to us soon. I anticipate that by the time 2022 nears the holidays, we will have witnessed a higher rate of growth in new breweries, forecasting that our state brewery count will hit sixty-five to sixty-eight breweries.

I am encouraged that there has been growth in the number of women brewers in our state,[4] with two new breweries celebrating great craft beer, brewed and served to you by talented brewers who happen to be women. Courtney Servaes, who owns Servaes Brewing Company in Shawnee, stood alone at the beginning of 2021 in our state. As the year closed, Deidre Knight from Riverbank Brewing in Council Grove and Kaydee Johnson and Laura Riggs-Johnson, who opened Ladybird Brewing in Winfield, have joined the Kansas craft beer community.

As I drove across the state, putting close to six thousand miles on our Honda Pilot, I fell in love with the views of barley and wheat fields ripe with growth, buffeted by the prairie winds, creating a visage of a prairie ocean. The experiences I enjoyed while driving state highways east, west, north and south made me think of two notable innovators in the Kansas beer agriculture scene.

Kansas Hop Company, situated in Ottawa, home to a three-acre hop farm, has become a significant supplier of hops to breweries, with close to 90 percent Kansas-based.[5] The team at Kansas Hop Company have had to be innovative, considering that hops need long daylight hours and more arable soil than can be found in Kansas. The number of Kansas breweries looking for state-grown hops is growing, as are the number of hop farms across the state. Brewers are keen to make beer with Kansas hops, including late fall introductions of wet hop or harvest beer. Kudos to these farms in our state that work with challenging growing conditions to make hop magic happen.

Close to 70 percent of the country's hops come from Oregon.[6] Great hops sourced from Oregon and Washington will continue to be used by our breweries. That does not mean that we cannot support and celebrate local, scanning tap menus for all-Kansas beer. Check out Blind Tiger, Willcott Brewing and Fields & Ivy, for starters.

Speaking of Fields & Ivy Brewery in Lawrence, owner Cory Johnston is an innovator worth watching as well. A goal for Cory is the ramping up of local grain utilization. Although Kansas is one of the top grain-growing regions in the world, the "brewing quality" of our grains needs to improve to make sure that world-class beer is made.

Cory and his wife, Veronica, own a 640-acre farm where wheat, barley and heirloom corn are grown. Fields & Ivy uses these grains in a variety of beers. He sees the upside in our state as the brewing community strengthens its reputation for innovative and high-quality beer. He continues to push for improvements, including securing a USDA grant allowing them to perform a feasibility study regarding the potential to build a malting facility in eastern Kansas.

The Kansas craft brewery industry has great opportunities to drive new innovations, illustrated through the two success stories here. At a point during our interview, Cory paused and said, "I wish I could predict where

Follow the sign for
the ice-cold beer.
Author's collection.

we go from here. We will try to grow in whatever way possible and continue to write the story of craft beer in Kansas."[7]

Cory is quoted on their brewery website for a statement that captures what could be next for our Sunflower State: "Kansas has long been the breadbasket of America, and we think it can be the beer barrel too."[8]

At this moment, as I share my last thoughts, I feel like I am at the edge of a pond once again. I have been throwing skipping stones as I write this book, hoping to witness multiple skips. The communities captured within each ring the sharp-edged stone has painted on the glassy surface of the pond will grow in the days ahead.

BREWERY APPENDIX

KANSAS BREWERY DIRECTORY (BREWERY NAME, MAP SECTION, MAP NUMBER AND CITY)

BLACK STAG BREWERY
Rock Chalk to Wildcat Country (no. 3)
Lawrence

BLIND TIGER BREWERY & RESTAURANT
Rock Chalk to Wildcat Country Section (no. 10)
Topeka

BLUE SKYE BREWERY & EATS
Smoky Hill Trail (no. 4)
Salina

BREW LAB BREWERY + KITCHEN
Ale Trail (no. 1)
Overland Park

CENTER PIVOT RESTAURANT & BREWERY
Smoky Hill Trail (no. 8)
Quinter

CENTRAL STANDARD BREWERY
The Wichita Way (no. 9)
Wichita

DEFIANCE BREWING COMPANY
Smoky Hill Trail (no. 6)
Hays

DODGE CITY BREWING
Santa Fe Trail (no. 1)
Dodge

DROP THE H BREWING COMPANY
Coal Fields to Little House on the Prairie (no. 2)
Pittsburg

DRY LAKE BREWERY
The Wichita Way (no. 1)
Great Bend

ExBEERIMENT
Ale Trail (no. 12)
Gardner

THE FARM
Smoky Hill Trail (no. 3)
Minneapolis

FIELDS & IVY BREWERY
Rock Chalk to Wildcat Country (no. 4)
Lawrence

15-24 BREW HOUSE
Rock Chalk to Wildcat Country Section (no. 17)
Clay Center

FLAT MOUNTAIN BREWHOUSE
Santa Fe Trail (no. 2)
Garden City

FLY BOY BREWERY & EATS
Smoky Hill Trail (no. 5)
Sylvan Grove

FREE STATE BREWING COMPANY
Rock Chalk to Wildcat Country (no. 1)
Lawrence

GELLA'S DINER & LB. BREWING COMPANY
Smoky Hill Trail (no. 7)
Hays

HANK IS WISER BREWERY
The Wichita Way (no. 12)
Cheney

HAPPY BASSET BREWING COMPANY
Rock Chalk to Wildcat Country (no. 11)
Topeka

HIDDEN TRAIL BREWERY
Santa Fe Trail (no. 3)
Garden City

HOPPING GNOME BREWING
The Wichita Way (no. 8)
Wichita

INDY BREW WORKS
Coal Fields to Little House on the Prairie (no. 3)
Independence

IRON RAIL BREWING COMPANY
Rock Chalk to Wildcat Country (no. 13)
Topeka

IRRIGATION ALES
Smoky Hill Trail (no. 2)
Courtland

JOLLY FOX BREWERY
Coal Fields to Little House on the Prairie (no. 1)
Pittsburg

KANSAS TERRITORY BREWING COMPANY
Rock Chalk to Wildcat Country (no. 19)
Washington

LADYBIRD BREWING
The Wichita Way (no. 13)
Winfield

LAWRENCE BEER COMPANY
Rock Chalk to Wildcat Country (no. 2)
Lawrence

LIMITLESS BREWING
Ale Trail (no. 9)
Lenexa

LOST EVENINGS BREWING COMPANY
Ale Trail (no. 8)
Lenexa

MANHATTAN BREWING COMPANY
Rock Chalk to Wildcat Country (no. 16)
Manhattan

NORSEMEN BREWING COMPANY
Rock Chalk to Wildcat Country (no. 9)
Topeka

NORTONS BREWING COMPANY
The Wichita Way (no. 6)
Wichita

NOT LOST BREWING COMPANY
Rock Chalk to Wildcat Country (no. 8)
Ottawa

OUTFIELD BEER COMPANY
Ale Trail (no. 13)
Bonner Springs

OZ BREWING
Smoky Hill Trail (no. 1)
Phillipsburg

PATHLIGHT BREWING
Ale Trail (no. 5)
Shawnee

RADIUS BREWING COMPANY
Rock Chalk to Wildcat Country (no. 14)
Emporia

RANGE 23 BREWING
Ale Trail (no. 14)
Kansas City Kansas

RED CROW BREWING COMPANY
Ale Trail (no. 10)
Olathe

RIVERBANK BREWING
Rock Chalk to Wildcat Country (no. 18)
Council Grove

RIVER CITY BREWING COMPANY
The Wichita Way (no. 11)
Wichita

ROCKCREEK BREWING COMPANY
Ale Trail (no. 3)
Mission

SALT CITY BREWING
The Wichita Way (no. 4)
Hutchinson

SANDHILLS BREWING
Ale Trail (no. 2)
Mission

SANDHILLS BREWING
The Wichita Way (no. 3)
Hutchinson

SERVAES BREWING COMPANY
Ale Trail (no. 4)
Shawnee

785 BEER COMPANY (2022 OPENING)
Rock Chalk to Wildcat Country Section (no. 12)
Topeka

TALL TRELLIS BREW CO
Ale Trail (no. 11)
Olathe

THIRD PLACE BREWING
The Wichita Way (no. 7)
Wichita

THREE RINGS BREWERY
The Wichita Way (no. 2)
McPherson

TRANSPORT BREWERY
Ale Trail (no. 6)
Shawnee

23RD STREET BREWERY
Rock Chalk to Wildcat Country Section (no. 5)
Lawrence

UNION WORKS BREWING COMPANY
Coal Fields to Little House on the Prairie (no. 4)
Humboldt

WALNUT RIVER BREWING COMPANY
The Wichita Way (no. 5)
El Dorado

WICHITA BREWING COMPANY
The Wichita Way (no. 10)
Wichita

WILLCOTT BREWING COMPANY
Rock Chalk to Wildcat Country (no. 15)
Holton

YANKEE TANK BREWING COMPANY
Rock Chalk to Wildcat Country (no. 6)
Lawrence

NOTES

Acknowledgements

1. J. Ryan Stradal, *The Lager Queen of Minnesota* (N.p.: Pamela Dorman Books, 2019).
2. Simron Khurana, "Irish Drinking Quotes for Your Next Toast," Irish Drinking Toasts and Quotes, January 4, 2020, liveabout.com.

Introduction

1. Brewers Association, State Craft Beer Sales & Production Statistics, 2020, brewersassociation.org.

Chapter 1

1. Wikipedia, "Library of Alexandria," https://en.wikipedia.org/wiki/Library_of_Alexandria.
2. Adam Rosdahl, Norsemen Brewing Company, Topeka, Kansas, June 19, 2021.
3. Brian C. Muraresku, *The Immortality Key: The Secret History of Religion with No Name* (New York: St. Martin's Press, 2020).
4. Rosdahl, Norsemen Brewing Company, June 19, 2021.
5. Ibid.
6. Ibid.
7. Ibid.

Chapter 2

1. BikeBrewQ, Great Bend, Kansas, www.bikebrewq.com.
2. Ryan Fairchild, Dry Lake Brewing, Great Bend, Kansas, September 3, 2021.
3. Brian Smith, "This Is Us," Three Rings Brewery, McPherson, Kansas, threeringsbrewery.com.
4. Wikipedia, "Martin Luther," https://en.wikipedia.org/wiki/Martin_Luther.
5. Ian Smith, Three Rings Brewery, McPherson, Kansas, October 20, 2021.
6. Ibid.
7. Pippin Williamson, Sandhills Brewing, Hutchinson, Kansas.
8. Side Project Brewing, Maplewood, Missouri, sideprojectbrewing.com.
9. Williamson, Sandhills Brewing.
10. Cole Petermann, Salt City Brewing Company, Hutchinson, Kansas, September 16, 2021.
11. Wikipedia, "Strataca," https://en.wikipedia.org/wiki/Strataca.
12. B.J. Hunt, Walnut River Brewing, El Dorado, Kansas, October 8, 2021.
13. Thomas Derstein, Homebrewer, El Dorado, Kansas, October 8, 2021.
14. Hunt, Walnut River Brewing.
15. Dan Norton, Nortons Brewing Company, Wichita, Kansas, January 10, 2022.
16. Ibid.
17. Ibid.
18. Ibid.
19. Ibid.
20. Ibid.
21. Ibid.
22. Tom Kryzer and Jason Algya, Third Place Brewing, Wichita, Kansas, July 31, 2021.
23. From William Shakespeare, *The Winter's Tale*, 1609–11.
24. Richard Sandomir, "M.T. Liggett, 86, Folk Artist and Provocateur, Is Dead," *New York Times*, August 23, 2017.
25. Cody Sherwood, Wichita Brewing Company, Wichita, Kansas, January 24, 2021.
26. Great American Beer Festival, "2021 GABF Winners," greatamerican beerfestival.com/the-competition/2021-GABF-winners.
27. Post by D.J., "2017 Great American Beer Festival Winners," Brew Public, October 8, 2017.
28. World Beer Cup, "2018 Award Winners," worldbeercup.org/press-releases/2018-world-beer-cup-winners-announced.
29. Sherwood, Wichita Brewing Company.

30. Chris Arnold, River City Brewing Company, Wichita, Kansas, January 10, 2021.
31. Brandon Fairs, River City Brewing Company, Wichita, Kansas, January 10, 2021.
32. Ibid.
33. E.B., "Hank Is Wiser Brewery: Great Beer, Great Food, Even Better People," *Wichita by EB*, August 7, 2018.
34. Steve Sanford, Hank Is Wiser Brewery, Cheney, Kansas.
35. Ibid.
36. Kaydee Johnson, Ladybird Brewing, Winfield, Kansas, October 7, 2021.
37. Ibid.
38. Ibid.
39. Brewers Association, "National Beer Sales & Production Data," brewersassociation.org.

Chapter 3

1. Geoff Deman, Free State Brewing Company, Lawrence, Kansas, September 24, 2021.
2. Ibid.
3. Brewers Association, "National Beer Sales & Production Data."
4. Deman, Free State Brewing Company.
5. Kendall Jones, "The Hops Capital of the World Is in Eastern Washington," *Seattle Magazine* (September 2017), seattlemag.com/news-and-features.
6. Deman, Free State Brewing Company.
7. Ibid.
8. Ibid.

Chapter 4

1. Deman, Free State Brewing Company.
2. Ibid.
3. Ibid.
4. Ibid.
5. Matt Williams, Lawrence Beer Company, Lawrence, Kansas, September 24, 2021.
6. Sam McClain, Lawrence Beer Company, Lawrence, Kansas, September 24, 2021.
7. Ibid.
8. Williams, Lawrence Beer Company.

9. Kathyrn Myers, Black Stag Brewery, Lawrence, Kansas, August 5, 2021.

10. Ibid.

11. Ibid.

12. Doug Bounds, "Kansas: A Leader in Wheat, Grain Sorghum, and Beef Production," USDA, July 29, 2021, USDA.gov/media/blog/2019/07/03.

13. Siebel Institute of Technology, siebelinstitute.com.

14. Dan Chivetta, Fields & Ivy Brewery, Lawrence, Kansas, September 27, 2021.

15. Ibid.

16. Ken Blanchard, "The One Minute Manager," *Berkley Trade*, February 15, 1986.

17. Ken Blanchard, *Raving Fans: A Revolutionary Approach to Customer Service* (N.p.: William Morrow, 1993).

18. Wikipedia, "Valhalla," https://en.wikipedia.org/wiki/Valhalla.

19. Brad Stevens, Brentwood, New Hampshire, June 18, 2021.

20. Adam Rosdahl, Norsemen Brewing Company, Topeka, Kansas, June 18, 2021.

21. Jared Rudy, Norsemen Brewing Company, Topeka, Kansas, June 18, 2021.

22. Brad Stevens, Brentwood, New Hampshire, June 18, 2021.

23. Rosdahl, Norsemen Brewing Company, June 18, 2021.

24. Nick Carr, "Kentucky Common: An Indigenous American Beer Style," Kegerator, January 8, 2018, learnkegerator.com/Kentucky-common.

25. Rosdahl, Norsemen Brewing Company, June 18, 2021.

26. John Dean, Blind Tiger Restaurant & Brewery, Topeka, Kansas, September 1, 2021.

27. Charlie Papazian, *The Complete Joy of Home Brewing* (New York: Avon, 1984).

28. Pete Dulin, "3 Must-Try Brews at Blind Tiger Brewery and Restaurant," *Feast Magazine* (February 27, 2015), feastmagazine.com/Kansas-city/article_3663129c.

29. Greater Topeka Hall of Foamers Home Brewing Club, Topeka, Kansas, Topekabrewers.com.

30. John Dean, Blind Tiger Restaurant & Brewery, Topeka, Kansas, September 1, 2021.

31. Ibid.

32. Ibid.

33. Ibid.

34. Ibid.

35. Luke Loewen, 785 Beer Company, Topeka, Kansas, January 26, 2022.

36. Ashley Loewen, 785 Beer Company, Topeka, Kansas, January 26, 2022.

37. Noah Oswald, Iron Rail Brewing, Topeka, Kansas, September 1, 2021.

38. Jeremy Johns, Radius Brewing Company, Emporia, Kansas, February 4, 2022.
39. Emporia Main Street, emporiamainstreet.com.
40. Johns, Radius Brewing Company.
41. Ibid.
42. Cindy Higgins, *Kansas Breweries & Beer* (N.p.: Ad Astra Press, 1992), 70–71.
43. Ibid., 71.
44. Johns, Radius Brewing Company.
45. Ibid.
46. Sean Willcott, Willcott Brewing Company, Holton, Kansas, October 13, 2021.
47. Ibid.
48. Ibid.
49. Ibid.
50. Ibid.
51. Ibid.
52. Ibid.
53. Wikipedia, "Manhattan Brewing Company of Chicago," https://en.wikipedia.org/wiki/Manhattan_Brewing_Company_of_Chicago.
54. Ivy Travis, Lawrence, Kansas, June 26, 2021.
55. Clint Armstrong, 15-24 Brew House, Clay Center, Kansas, June 27, 2021.
56. Ibid.
57. Ibid.
58. Allman Brothers Band, *Eat a Peach*, Capricorn, 1972, via lyrics.rockmagic.com.
59. Armstrong, 15-24 Brew House.
60. Ibid.
61. Deidre Knight, Riverbank Brewing, Council Grove, Kansas, September 2, 2021.
62. Ibid.
63. Laura Kiniry, "The 15 Best Small Towns to Visit in 2021," *Smithsonian* (June 7, 2021), smithsonianmag.com.
64. Brad Portenier, Kansas Territory Brewing Company, Washington, Kansas, October 14, 2021.
65. Ibid.
66. Ibid.
67. Ibid.

Chapter 5

1. Sam McClain, Lawrence Beer Company, Lawrence, Kansas, September 24, 2021.
2. Ibid.
3. Ibid.
4. Ibid.
5. Ibid.
6. Ibid.
7. Ibid.
8. Ibid.

Chapter 6

1. Alexandra Hicks, "Hop Along the JoCo Ale Trail," *City Lifestyle Kansas City*, citylifestyle.com/Kansas-city-mo/articles.
2. Kevin Combs, Brew Lab Brewery, Overland Park, Kansas, January 29, 2022.
3. Charley Olson, Brew Lab Brewery, Overland Park, Kansas, January 29, 2022.
4. Combs, Brew Lab Brewery.
5. Ibid.
6. Courtney Servaes, Servaes Brewing Company, Shawnee, Kansas, September 15, 2022.
7. Ibid.
8. Ibid.
9. Lawrence Brewers Guild, lawrencebrewers.org.
10. Wikipedia, "Synesthesia," https://en.wikipedia.org/wiki/Synesthesia.
11. Tanner Vaughn, Pathlight Brewing, Shawnee, Kansas, July 16, 2021.
12. Meaghan Travis, Lawrence, Kansas, July 16, 2021.
13. World Population Review, Johnson County population growth, worldpopulationreview.com/us-counties/Kansas/johnson-county-population.
14. Pat Davis, Lost Evenings Brewing Company, Lenexa, Kansas, September 30, 2021.
15. Frank Turner, "I Knew Prufrock Before He Got Famous," AZ Lyrics, AZlyrics.com/lyrics/frankturner.
16. Emily Mobley, Limitless Brewing, Lenexa, Kansas, September 15, 2021.
17. Ibid.
18. Misty Roberts, Red Crow Brewing Company, Olathe, Kansas, January 14, 2022.

19. Chris Roberts, Red Crow Brewing Company, Olathe, Kansas, January 14, 2022.
20. Misty Roberts, Red Crow Brewing Company.
21. Ryan Triggs, Tall Trellis Brew Co, Olathe, Kansas, September 22, 2021.
22. Ibid.
23. Kansas Hop Company, Ottawa, Kansas, kansashopco.com.
24. Triggs, Tall Trellis Brew Co.
25. Nick Feightner, Tall Trellis Brew Co, Olathe, Kansas, September 22, 2021.
26. Misty Eytcheson, ExBEERiment, Gardner, Kansas, September 8, 2021.
27. Ibid.
28. Ibid.
29. Beau Martin, Outfield Beer Company, Bonner Springs, Kansas, August 13, 2021.
30. Ibid.
31. Karen Schotanus, Range 23 Brewing, Kansas City, Kansas, July 8, 2021.
32. Wikipedia, "Public Land Survey System," https://en.wikipedia.org/wiki/Public_Land_Survey_System.

Chapter 7

1. Steve Nicholson, Center Pivot Restaurant & Brewery, Quinter, Kansas, June 4, 2021.
2. Ibid.
3. Ibid.
4. Kathy Weiser-Alexander, "Smoky Hill Trail, Kansas—Heading for Gold," Legends of America, June 2021, legendsofamerica.com/ks-smokyhilltrail.
5. Nicholson, Center Pivot Restaurant & Brewery.

Chapter 8

1. Luke Mahin, Irrigation Ales, Courtland, Kansas, August 28, 2021.
2. Marci Penner, "Kansas Power Up & Go: The Action Report," Kansas Sampler Foundation & the Office of Rural Prosperity, May 2021, kansassampler.org.
3. Kansas Bostwick Irrigation District, Kansas Department of Agriculture, agriculture.ks.gov/division-programs.
4. Luke Mahin, Irrigation Ales, Courtland, Kansas, August 28, 2021.
5. Jennifer Mahin, Irrigation Ales, Courtland, Kansas, August 28, 2021.
6. Ashley Swisher, The Farm, Minneapolis, Kansas, December 14, 2021.

7. Kyle Banman, The Farm, Minneapolis, Kansas, December 14, 2021.

8. Keir Swisher, The Farm, Minneapolis, Kansas, December 14, 2021.

9. Lucas Hass, Fly Boy Brewery & Eats, Sylvan Grove, Kansas.

10. Ibid.

11. Ibid.

12. Matt Bender, Defiance Brewing Company, Hays, Kansas, June 4, 2021.

13. Dylan Seltzer, Defiance Brewing Company, Hays, Kansas, June 4, 2021.

14. Ibid.

15. Bender, Defiance Brewing Company.

16. Ibid.

17. Ibid.

18. Higgins, *Kansas Breweries & Beer*, 76–77.

19. Ryan Engel, Gella's Diner + Lb. Brewing Company, Hays, Kansas, July 8, 2021.

20. Ibid.

21. Ibid.

22. Nicholson, Center Pivot Restaurant & Brewery.

Chapter 10

1. Larry Cook, Dodge City Brewing, Dodge City, Kansas, June 3, 2021.

2. Ibid.

3. Ibid.

4. Ibid.

5. Ibid.

6. Jude Cundiff, Hidden Trail Brewing, Garden City, Kansas, August 27, 2021.

7. Michael Cole, Hidden Trail Brewing, Garden City, Kansas, August 27, 2021.

8. Cody Cundiff, Hidden Trail Brewing, Garden City, Kansas, August 27, 2021.

Chapter 11

1. Toby Keith, "Peso in My Pocket," *Peso in My Pocket*, Show Dog–Universal Music, December 10, 2021.

2. Marci Penner, Kansas Sampler Foundation, Inman, Kansas, October 25, 2021.

3. Penner, "Kansas Power Up & Go."

4. Tracy Henry, Greater Morris County Development, Council Grove, Kansas, November 4, 2021.

5. Ibid.
6. Jennifer M. Kassebaum, Flint Hills Books, Council Grove, Kansas.
7. NetWork Kansas, networkkansas.com.
8. Keith, "Peso in My Pocket."
9. Jesse Knight, Riverbank Brewing, Council Grove, Kansas, September 2, 2021.
10. Lindsay Gant, Riverbank Brewing, Council Grove, Kansas, September 2, 2021.
11. Deidre Knight, Riverbank Brewing, Council Grove, Kansas, September 2, 2021.
12. Jesse Knight, Riverbank Brewing.
13. Penner, "Kansas Power Up & Go."
14. Henry, Greater Morris County Development.
15. Penner, "Kansas Power Up & Go."
16. Penner, Kansas Sampler Foundation
17. Ibid.
18. Penner, "Kansas Power Up & Go."
19. Keith, "Peso in My Pocket."
20. Penner, "Kansas Power Up & Go."

Chapter 12

1. Joel Stewart, The Jolly Fox Brewery, Pittsburg, Kansas, August 13, 2021.
2. Ibid.
3. Ibid.
4. Wikipedia, "Durant Motors," https://en.wikipedia.org/wiki/Durant_Motors.
5. Mark McClain, Drop the H Brewery, Pittsburg, Kansas, January 17, 2022.
6. Craft Sense, "What Is Germany's Beer Purity Law (Reinheitsgebot) About?," craftsense.co/craft-beverage.
7. McClain, Drop the H Brewery.
8. Wikipedia, "Humboldt, Kansas," https://en.wikipedia.org/wiki/Humboldt,_Kansas.
9. Tony Works, Union Works Brewing Company, Humboldt, Kansas, July 6, 2021.
10. Ibid.
11. Ibid.
12. Ibid.

Afterword

1. Brewers Association, State Craft Beer Sales & Production Statistics, 2020.
2. Brewers Association, National Beer Sales & Production Data, brewersassociation.org.
3. Brewers Association, State Craft Beer Sales & Production Statistics, 2020.
4. Jason Murphy, "5 Questions with Women's Craft Beer Collective Founder Kristine Baker," Porch Drinking, January 7, 2022, porchdrinking.com/articles.
5. Brianne Childers, "Kansas Farmers Are Making Hops into Crops. They Are Defying the Odds of Heavy Soil and Less Daylight," *Topeka Capital-Journal*, April 24, 2021.
6. Ibid.
7. Cory Johnston, Fields & Ivy Brewery, Lawrence, Kansas.
8. Ibid.

ABOUT THE AUTHOR

Michael Travis first fell in love with beer while attending the University of New Hampshire in the early 1980s. His dad bet a case of beer on the UNH versus Lehigh annual football game with a dear friend and work associate. Frank Travis, a UNH alum, put a case of Budweiser (brewed in Merrimack, New Hampshire) on the line, while his friend Mike, a Lehigh graduate, ponied up a case of Rolling Rock. Michael carried free cases of the iconic green bottles back to his dorm two of his four years at UNH, returning a hero. He graduated with a BA in economics, studying important supply and demand theories, learning to take advantage of heavily inventoried, inexpensive beer brands perfect to quench a college kid's thirst.

The author enjoying a beer and pondering life in Lawrence. *Courtesy of Jason Dailey, photo + motion, Lawrence, Kansas.*

Michael worked in corporate retail for years, starting with Target in Minneapolis, birthplace of both daughters. He learned to appreciate the art and effort put into gourmet food, exquisite wine and great craft beer during his career spent primarily with Payless Shoesource in Topeka, Kansas. Michael is blessed to have a wonderful wife, Ivy, who has graced him with her wisdom and love since they fell in love at UNH at the tender ages of nineteen. The two live close to their beautiful daughters, Katie and Meaghan, who are creating their own wonderful lives.

The pandemic years forced Michael to redefine his professional career, after losing a position in the first year that COVID struck. He established a retail consulting company catering to small businesses. This new venture gave him the freedom to chase a dream, becoming another Travis sibling in pursuit of telling stories. He followed in the footsteps of his mother, Marty, and his two brothers, Mark and Phil, who have shared their writing, whether it be a Civil War history, meditations about life and its struggles or heartfelt and experimental poetry.

Michael declared that it was his time to tell a story. He celebrates the spiral-bound journal he wrote, capturing a 1972 family summer road trip to the West Coast and back, by seeing *Celebrating Kansas Breweries: People, Places and Stories* be published fifty years later.